UNDER THEIR WINGS

PATTY LOU HAWKS

Made for Success
PUBLISHING

Made for Success Publishing P.O. Box 1775 Issaquah, WA 98027

Library of Congress Cataloging-in-Publication data Hawks, Patty Lou., date, Under Their Wings: A Daring Adventure Mentoring Girls / Patty Lou Hawks.
p. cm.
ISBN-13: 9781613398661 (pbk.)
LCCN: 2016906523

To contact the author or publisher please email service@MadeforSuccess.net or call +1 425 657 0300.

Made for Success Publishing is an imprint of Made for Success, Inc.

Printed in the United States of America

This book is dedicated to:

Sally, Kathy and Crystal
Who served tirelessly, selflessly, and endlessly with me to lift up the girls!

And MOST importantly,
The Girls of Troop 145

With Special Thanks to the girls that "hung on" to the
end - Heather, Kelcy, Chelsea, Danica and Erin

You are all my Heroes!

To Jessica,

Blessings & Aloha's,

Patty Lou Hawks

TABLE OF CONTENTS

FOREWORD

BEFORE YOU CONTINUE reading this book, I would like to thank you for adding this book to your life, and becoming a part of the journey. Every person has a purpose and a journey of their own, and I just wanted to say thank you for letting us share ours.

Growing up you never know where life is going to take you or what it all means in the present moment, but as we trust in God, He slowly reveals His plan for us. When I was younger, all I wanted to be was a Girl Scout, not because I knew how it would transform me into the diverse, hard-working, joyful woman that I am today, but because it looked like fun! Plus, I got to be around my friends, go on exciting outings, learn new things about life, and serve others. Although all these great qualities attracted me to Girl Scouts, I never realized how hard it would be to stay committed.

Then one day my mom decides to write a book about it. Maybe if I had known that, I would have acted differently. And if my mother had asked me to write this when I was 12, I would have gone on about how she was the worst leader ever! Truth be told, as cute and adorable as my mother makes me out to be, that wasn't always the case. Most of the time I was the worst scout out of the troop.

The commitment to Girl Scouts was hard for the whole family. We had to create an environment for 12 girls at our house once a week, preparing for crafts, snacks, activities, and hikes. Girls came and went from our troop, some would leave and rejoin. I even disliked Girl Scouts at one point and wanted to quit, most of us did. But my mom continued to push us and encourage us to stick it out for one more year, and then one more, and one more, and another, and then it became fun again!

To the mothers and troop leaders reading this book, this is coming from a girl who was, at times, as stubborn as a mule. I write this in hopes that you don't give up on your daughter or her troop. I am so thankful that our leader, my mother, never allowed giving up to be an option. I encourage you to continue to act out of love, empower the young women in your life to be the "best girl" she can be at all times, and she WILL thank you.

I didn't notice how much my mother sacrificed for me. It's not an easy path, but it is the only path that reaps truth, purity, and a good life. Honestly, as we work, share, and continue on a solid road together, we will make a difference in this world, and make it a better place.

Thank you for being a part of the story.
With Aloha!
Heather

PREFACE

THE ARTISTRY OF words within this text is about my daughter and her friends and reveals the meaning of life through a child's eyes in a beautiful waltz of learning and discovery. The events take place over a ten-year span beginning with kindergarten and through the high school years. The epic journey begins in a small beach town on the windward coast of Oahu, postulating the daily struggles of living life and raising a family, surrounded by the start-up of a Girl Scout troop.

The nostalgic stories are interwoven with Hawaiian culture, growing pains, rites of passage, and my personal thoughts observing adolescent behaviors. While spending time together, there are naturally bonding moments, self-realizations, epiphanies, and successes with surprising results along the path.

The original journals developed as a memoir keepsake for my daughter, which later took on new life by adding in all the back stories with a charming cast of characters encountered during our experiences; thus, lending insight and unique dimensions, rich with humor and wisdom. The final draft finally flew off the shelf one last time with a breath of fresh air reflecting on the entire process, while listening to an inspiring talk by Seattle Seahawks quarterback Russell Wilson.

During a media interview, Russell shared about a talk he had with his teammates before walking onto the playing field of his first Super Bowl showdown. Using the gift of words imparted by his late father, he conversed about a thought process which had instilled calmness, confidence, and self-esteem early on in his childhood. Basically, the message his father conveyed was, in life give it all you've got, do your very best, and then adopt the phrase, "Why Not You?" In other words, if someone's going to have it, win it, do it, be it, why not you?!

The message was abundantly powerful all on its own. However, he communicated the meaning with such passion and conviction, "Why not you Russell? If it's going to be someone, why not let it be you?" Later, he reconnects the message with his teammates, and they held the mantra, "Why Not Us?" all the way to victory; winning the 48th Super Bowl in 2014.

Hearing his words unfold in his story lit a flame in me once again to retrieve this book off the shelf, knowing it had to be completed for publication. There was still a missing link, and Russell's message inspired and connected the "Aha!" moment I had been waiting for to adequately wrap up my final thoughts, insights, and reflections.

Taking a second look at the opening chapter titled "Why Me?" while examining the final results, it truly gave me the word with the meaning I needed to finish the manuscript. It was as simple as just one word, and that word was NOT. Reflecting on the opening chapter, what I should have been asking was, "Why NOT Me?" vs. "Why Me?" What a difference one word makes! It changes everything from attitude to gratitude and everything in between. Going from victim to victor all by adding one word! It can take you from over thinking it too much to trusting and letting go. Letting go and letting God, if you will.

Trusting there may be a better plan by simply learning how to "let go" of the controls, and waiting patiently to see how life unfolds! This was one of the many lessons I eventually learned along the journey. It truly is such a simple, yet powerful process which goes on in life simultaneously, while we're living it and learning it all at the same time. Being caught up in the swift moments of life is perhaps why it's too overwhelming to see until later.

Lastly, while trusting in the process on the entire journey, it's very apropos to find the final link or word connecting all my thoughts and reflections from a gentleman who caught my attention with the phrase "Go Hawks!" Poignant because I've never watched football. However, it caught my attention because it is my last name. It was significant because I titled the book *Under Their Wings*, and befitting that the final reflections of this story be revealed "under the wings" of one of the Hawks.

This book began as a journal over twenty years ago, intended as a gift for my daughter about our journey together while becoming her Girl Scout leader. It is dedicated to her and the girls of Troop 145 who graciously and lovingly encouraged me (along with urging from friends, family, and clients) and who felt these lessons, through story, should be shared with others for a higher purpose.

So, from here the story goes with all the ups and downs on the path, with moments that are raw, rare, eye-opening and heartwarming, but they are never dull or without a lesson for me or the girls. My journey with them will be some of my finest hours ever spent in life, and I am eternally honored and grateful for having the privilege of taking the trip with them.

I am just as honored to have met and worked with some of the greatest adult individuals along the way who supported, helped, mentored or touched our lives in some special way; it really does take a village to properly raise up a child. I am and will forever be grateful for the village that supported me in lifting up these girls. Equipping them in life with self-esteem, kindness, bravery, courage, creativity, honesty, benevolence, and self-respect, as well as respect for others, life, animals and our planet.

What a world we would have to live in if every child could grow up and experience these elements in a safe and healthy environment. I dream of that world often! A world where humans gift their offspring with the proper tools and messages for navigating life in an abundantly healthy way. I envision our society evolving and elevating the planet with a higher consciousness and mission with our youth at the center. I see all of us able to love one another without judgments or conditions, to serve without abandon, and to protect all on the planet without question or ceasing.

I did my very best to emulate, create, and pass on as many of these attributes as possible to these amazing young women who were specially placed on my path. And now I give them (and the world) this book as a tribute, for all they mean to me, for all they have done, have yet to do, and will do in their lives while passing the torch. I especially want to thank them for being so patient and understanding with me, while I learned and practiced life with them.

Respectfully shared and given with Aloha, Miss Pat

CHAPTER 1
WHY ME?

I WAS STANDING AT the back of my daughter's school cafeteria for an evening meeting, listening to a redhead, freckle-faced woman reverberating into a microphone, and trying to ascertain what she was saying. Echoes of screaming children bounced off the walls, drowning out the poor sound of the PA system. My daughter, Heather, was at a craft table not more than a few feet away from me.

I was more captivated by the art projects and watched endearingly as my little half pint maneuvered the huge bottle of glue that went way beyond her kindergarten years. Her tiny little hands worked intently on the task, focusing like a cat watching for prey. The white liquid seemed to flow onto the paper synchronized with her tongue sliding in and out between the two missing front teeth. She had me at, "Look mommy at what I can do!"

"Don't buy it," murmured the woman standing at attention to my right, cupping her hand around one side of her mouth, obviously directing the comment for my ears only. I spun around quickly to see if I knew the face that matched the voice. She was a petite-framed woman with an athletic build, coming up to my shoulder at about 5'2" with a dark brown, Dorothy Hamel haircut that matched her playful brown eyes, yet I still drew a blank.

Turning to get a better view, I responded, "Pardon?" Leaving a question mark hanging in the air, with a squinty-eyed expression that said *what did you just say?*

Grinning like the Cheshire cat, she giggled while emerging her hand in a familiar greeting, "Hi, I'm Sally." With a firm grip and a quick shake, we both burst into laughter about the opening introductions. She continued without much hesitation, "Be very careful here, they are trying to pull you in."

"Pull me in?" I repeated, still leaving a question mark hanging mid-sentence.

She looked around our immediate vicinity, leaned in just a bit closer, and lowered her voice, "I'm just saying, they are looking to recruit troop leaders here tonight, and that's how they do it," pointing towards the busy craft tables. She continued with her advanced knowledge, warning me, "Just don't volunteer for anything, or once they find out what your weaknesses are, they'll have you working full-time for slave labor." We both burst into laughter about the exaggerated implications, this time with an unspoken understanding of being pulled in by a mother's heart strings.

Then she motioned towards her older daughter, Megan, who was assisting the younger girls with art projects, and said, "I've been here before, and they can pull you in." Chuckling again at her candor, we settled into a more serious conversation about our own scouting experiences as children, reminiscing about the fun we most certainly had, and ultimately agreeing about the usefulness of our shared experiences.

We wrapped the conversation with laments about how it was different for mothers to become leaders back in the day. After all, when we were children, our mothers stayed home full-time, while most of the moms in our generation were out of the house working full-time careers. After opening this door of life in the conversation, I chimed in a bit more, elaborating about the dynamics of my overly busy family life and inflamed work schedule. "I have four children at home, volunteer at my church, serve on the school board, help with the Boy Scouts, and manage a hairstyling business, while my husband travels for work." I reassured her I would not be stepping up to the plate to volunteer for any new positions tonight or any other night.

She merely laughed at my attempts for solidarity, folding her arms across her chest and turning towards the oration at the front of the room. We both giggled on cue as she tilted her head sideways supporting her opening sentiments while we turned to listen to the closing platform, "I'm just saying, don't volunteer for anything. A-N-Y-T-H-I-N-G, I tell you."

With a newly formed union and kinship from the back of the room, I found it much easier to slip out a side door without as much as signing up to be a snack helper, only to be confronted on the way to the car by my favorite little midget friend with her art piece and irresistible toothless smile. I'd almost forgotten she was the reason I was attending this meeting in the first place.

While loading, and buckling her into the car, visions of her running in after school earlier that day flooded my memory banks, and I could still see her racing all the way home from the bus stop. She dashed into the door of my salon, located on the side of our house, waving the flyer and breathlessly bellowing, "Mommy! Mommy! We must go tonight! It's tonight, and we *have* to go! My friends are going, I wanna go! Can we go?!"

Her appeals to enlist me as a troop leader lasted all the way home and well into the bedtime rituals. She had such a theatrical way of tilting her head sideways like a sad, little puppy dog and curling out her lower lip to get what she wanted, and she knew exactly how to work it. I was pretty much immune to her academy award performances by this age, but somehow, this time, it was different. *How is she getting to me so easily?* I thought. Or, perhaps more significantly, *why is she getting to me so easily?*

I couldn't decipher these questions on my toes at the end of the day and had to press on, winding down the evening with a whole lot of lip service to get through the bedtime routine. I bounced her into bed avoiding her irresistible, saucer brown eyes, knowing they could penetrate my soul and move heaven and earth to get past all reason and logic.

However, I could not get past the little chirping sounds that were like pin pricks jabbing at my heart, "But Mommy, Mommy, pleeeeeeeze. We can't be a Girl Scout troop if we don't have a leader; why can't youuuu be a leader? Pleeeeeeeeeze Momma! I wanna be a Girl Scout with my friends."

"We will talk about this tomorrow," I assured with hugs and kisses, tucking covers around her like a mummy and quickly retreating to the living room to lick my wounds. Sinking into my cherished, feather-down chair, I sipped my unique blend of honey and herb tea and tried letting the day pass. However, my brainwaves had another idea and were in full throttle mode without a shift mechanism to locate neutral. I closed my eyes and tried relaxing with meditation when my inner Yoda began interrupting with her own common sense opinions, "Stop trying so hard, and do."

To no avail, guilt toiled its way back in, disturbing my peaceful state of mind. Much like a bullhorn attached to a tape recorder, I replayed my schedule and list of justifications as to why I could not take on one more task in my life. Worse yet, I couldn't seem to stop answering these self-imposed deliberations.

Silent arguments kept churning deep within my being until they waged a full-on civil war with my core beliefs. The internal festering could no longer be ignored with questions going off like sirens in my senses, shrieking the overall prevailing thought, *why won't this just go away? You have said no before without this kind of reaction.*

But the hard follow-up question that really got stuck in my craw was, *what is it? What's really bugging you about all of this?*

Intuitively, I knew there was no way out except to scrutinize these thoughts in order. Nevertheless, I wasn't particularly enthralled with delving any deeper into the abyss, where my truths and accuracies were firmly lying entrenched, dormant and quiet for now. However, the questions igniting by the milliseconds in the gray matter of my mind, like exploding popcorn, had other ideas.

With nowhere else to go, except down the rabbit hole for answers, the fifty-thousand-dollar question lit up the circuit boards, *what are you so afraid of looking at?* And there it was, the big white elephant sitting in the middle of the room that nobody wanted to talk about: *Fear!* What's that all about?

I tried desperately to avoid looking for these answers by coming up with provisional questions like, *how can I save face with my adorable, little, brown-eyed munchkin, without adding one more task to the endless list?* That was the cover-up question I was willing to see or work on, with a veiled attempt to suppress the real undercurrent issues of dealing with my fears. After all, opening this door too suddenly could produce a tidal wave of emotions.

Yes, denial runs deep while using a heavy cloak to mask the spiny tentacles digging multi-layers into the psyche, in which the real issues hide. However, I stayed the course, ignoring the jabs of repudiation, and explored these feelings smoldering just beneath the surface, which lingered somewhere between guilt and anger.

Ruminating in this lonely valley for a few more minutes, my deliberations finally shifted into high gear with attitudes of resentment. Raising the even deeper questions of, resentment over what? For being in this situation in the first place? Or, was the resentment just a result of frustration for even having to make such a difficult decision?

Each reflection brought up new examinations, along with more frustration and even more questions like, *are you really justified in your self-preserving "no?"* and, *why are you being so defensive about simply saying "no?"* Continuing the silent debate, I tried justifications to profoundly cover it up again, but, denial ain't just a river in Egypt, and I felt much safer floating down the river than listening to my own subconscious screaming these questions and, more importantly, the answers.

However, the inner voice would not be squelched this time, and the self-inquiries firing now would need more than a fire extinguisher to douse them. *Are you truly being honest with yourself? Are you resentful of the situation, or the fact that you have to make the decision?* asked my inner voice, now getting down to the nittygritty points, *or is the resentment based on the fact that without the luxury of time, you can't make the decision you truly desire, following a path you dearly want to take?*

Digging deep enough and being perfectly honest with myself, I knew exactly what it was! I wanted to be more involved with my daughter's activities and her life; however, I wasn't making the time or making it my priority. Was it because I couldn't find the time? Did I have this luxury of time where I could be more involved? Was I just exaggerating with excuses? After examining these interrogations and looking for more precision, I found some burdensome conclusions.

However, the most difficult analysis was admitting that I needed to be more honest with myself. In all honesty, it wasn't so much the resentment of the decision I had to make, but more the fact that I hadn't planned my life and activities around having the luxury of time to do what my heart really and truly desired or wanted to be doing. The frustrations set in when I started juggling my heart's desire with my life's reality.

I tried to let it all in at once. However, the facts remained the facts, and honesty didn't get rid of my full laundry list of things to do in the immediate future. I had backed myself into this corner of life with a large family, a huge home, career choices, other volunteer positions, and I had to see them through before I could otherwise reorganize and reprioritize the lists of my life.

Still banging my head against a wall, I enumerated and recited the list, hashing it over and over again for the next several days to anyone who would listen, "I have four children at home, two of which are going to junior high and high school, both involved in sports, Boy Scouting, music, church youth group, and I am serving on the school board, running a hairstyling business with a demanding clientele, taking care of a house, a yard, a zoo full of pets, and I CAN'T possibly take on one more thing." I would recite this almost as if I were defending my choices or trying to invoke sympathy, while outwardly posturing a state of denial.

My husband usually caught the brunt of it to which he would simply reply, "I know you can't do it and don't look at me for any help, I'm already doing the carpooling for sports, helping with the Boy Scouts and running my own business."

A week later, out of the blue, my laments were finally alleviated with a call from another mom stepping up to volunteer as the leader. We now had a Daisy Scout troop starting up with meetings beginning in a week. The news immediately thrilled Heather into turning cartwheels, with roars of triumph and victory. Watching her excitement over the news further deepened my guilt, denial, and resentment. I simply let it go with the conjured smile we busy moms have grown accustomed to wearing while getting back to business as usual.

It was a welcome relief to see my new friend Sally and her daughter Kelcy at the first meeting, along with eight other anxious, giggly girls and their moms. It was a virtual bouncy house of infectious laughter and terminal cuteness thriving at every angle. It doesn't require a huge scientific study to prove we are social beings.

Simply put eight giggling girls in a room with food, games, and crafts for an hour and — voilà — there is actual proof of this natural human phenomenon! It is also not possible to have this kind of fun and amusement without a group situation. Hence, the excitement over having a Girl Scout troop.

I enjoyed their folly and uncontrollable excitement almost as much as they did. My heart soared merely watching them make new friends, learning new songs, dancing and prancing about, creating their own fun and merriment. It candidly felt surreal, like I was reliving my own childhood while contributing a sense of value to my life. These connections complemented my inherent nature and felt like I was finally dwelling in my zone.

Yes, it was therapeutic, and I loved watching them romp like a litter of pups in high weeds. It resonated within my core, like pouring cool water over hot embers, to see them so full of life. They were like sponges absorbing new things, and ready to take on the world. While being amused with their beginnings at this impressionable age, I realized I wanted the best for them and believed, in many ways, I was also afraid of them.

I believed the internal dialog had stifled me for a brief time and watching them socialize now I realized the turmoil still lingered just beneath the surface. Only shrouded secretly in a place where I dreamed for more liberty with my time to be more involved in my daughter's life and her activities. With all honesty looking inward at the most profound level, I wasn't just suffering from the fear of taking on too much or doing too many tasks. If that was true and genuinely a concern, then why did I already have such a full list of tasks already at my fingertips? No, being busy and doing too much was not on my radar of deepest fears!

Burrowing down to the innermost personal space, I took another look. I knew there was more fear associated with taking on the responsibility of shaping their young lives than the fear of a hectic schedule. What if things didn't go right, or heaven forbid, what if I didn't do it perfect? Then what? Yes, playing it safe and not taking it on at all meant I couldn't mess it up! Someone else could hold that great distinction, and I would be off the hook! This new vein of honesty was really starting to chap my hiney and felt like I couldn't get it off the proverbial hot seat.

Within a fleeting hour, their playtime and my reflections were over, and it was back to the world of reality. Jumping out of the catbird seat for now and dusting off the ashes, Sally and I congratulated each other for holding our ground by not taking on more than we could handle. This meant we could go back to our busy lives, let go of our guilt, and help out occasionally with the troop. The first year vanished quickly with our busy schedules, as mother time seems to do when one constantly stays busy and on the go. Before we knew what hit us, we were at a graduation party with the girls bridging up to Brownies!

In true Hawaiian style, all the families gathered for the celebration at the leader's clubhouse pool. We commemorated our new family bonds and friendships with a potluck, games, music, and fun in the sun, ending the party with a ceremony of pomp and circumstance. Each girl walked over a portable bridge meeting her parents and the leader to receive their distinguished Brownie Wings, flying up and becoming full-fledged Brownie Scouts. Puffed out chests and toothless smiles reigned in the day with a photo finish around the pool of course.

As quickly as the year began, it was now time for a muchneeded summer break. No one wanted to say goodbye for the recess, yet somehow we all needed to step back and take a little breather. Yes, we all definitely made new friends, experienced many new adventures, but most importantly we all had *fun* in the process!

*

Later during the summer, we learned the newly formed troop would need to find another leader if they were to continue on as a Brownie troop in the fall. We were back at square one, readdressing all our demanding time agendas, inner turmoil, and resetting the priorities list!

My first response was *no*! Hordes of thoughts and questions filled my monkey brain again. However, this time, there was no brushing them off, and nothing would ever quell the persistent feelings pulsating from these subjects except to dive right in. I worried about the struggle to find a balance for holding it all together. I worried incessantly about how we would pay all the bills, adjust the schedules, take care of our marriage, the kids, their education, my work, my health, the family's health, the house, the pets...the list never seemed to have an end, and I was perpetually looking for answers!

I sat in this lonely place of contemplation and meditation until opting for an old standby practice of picking up a Bible and randomly reading a page. In times of struggle, feeling lost, or looking for answers, I would crack it open to a spontaneous page and see what the universe had to convey. As fate would have it, splayed open on the pages lying in front of me was a confirmation to sit up and listen. Randomly landing on the passages about Moses, when God called on him to deliver his people from bondage.

I'm not suggesting my dilemma or story was anything like Moses'. However, while reading the scriptures, I could certainly commiserate and relate with Moses answering God's call with, "No, this is not me, this is not who you want. Go find someone stronger, smarter, and more gifted, I am just not capable of taking on such an important task." This was truly how I felt and how I was answering a call to simply step up and lead a Girl Scout troop.

Sitting quietly and listening, I heard the answers being expressed within my subconscious attention. It kept calling or nagging as it were, for me to sit still and wait for the colloquies to answer. "Listen to me," it said. "This is you, and I will walk you through this one, one step at a time, just pick up the baton and pass on what you already know; it will all come together somehow, and I will give you what you need when you need it."

From within my gut, I knew I had to take a leap of faith, trust the process with taking care of everything, and simply throw out the worry list. I had to be more conscious and in the moment because this truly was all I had any control of anyway. When I realized my actual struggle was with my inner soul trying to be heard, I knew exactly what the answer was.

I got out of my own way and permitted my inner voice to clearly have a say. Realizing the source of all my physical pain and self-imposed conflicts could easily be cured by opening the channels to simply hear my own intuition. It was full of expression, and the very minute I stopped these internal battles, like a dam breaking, all my answers flowed and spewed from many different sources, but mostly from within.

I finally heard the answer I had been trying so hard to quell saying, "*You* want this, *you* got this, now make it happen, *you make the time*. This daughter of yours is one of your most prized gifts!"

Yes, back to square one, we needed a leader to keep the girls together and on a strong path. Someone who would go the course, mentor them and be a strong role-model. Someone who could build trust, continuity, and ultimately lead leaders. Not just leaders of our communities, but leaders of self first. Young girls and women need to be leaders of self in order to make the right choices and decisions when life smacks them upside the head. They will also need lots of love through this sensitive, complicated process.

Having many new revelations, and finally wanting to step up to the plate, I still didn't have all the confidence I required for taking on the role of a leader. While the scariest part wasn't only the need for mustering more confidence, I still had the mandatory juggling act of family schedules, work agendas, taking care of a home and other volunteer responsibilities. After fixing the time constraints, and figuring out how we could pay all our bills, I had to complete three levels of leader training classes all by the end of summer.

Needless to say, I was feeling the crushing throes of overwhelm coupled with the distinct honor and pleasure of being blessed and born in the year of the monkey (with a scattered monkey brain to go with it) where self-doubts and never-ending lists and questions were setting up camp and building strip malls in my head.

Even questioning thoughts like: *Where does this self-doubt come from?* or, *will it ever go away?* Then moving on to, *now what do I need to move, give up or juggle to take on a Girl Scout troop?* and *How will I make this all work?* The short-term answer that I came up with quickly was to give up sleep.

Learning to trust myself and my intuition with these situations became the most difficult and yet the most invaluable lesson I learned throughout the journey. Eventually, I also learned how to train and harness this monkey brain of mine. Thank the Lord we didn't have the media technology of today's world or I probably wouldn't have survived the rabble-rousers or interruptions with battles of divided attention.

I had to find stellar focus, filtering out the unnecessary data and questions coming at me daily, just so I could actually hear the more important messages trying to refine and sift their way in like, "this is what you need to do," or, "this needs to be done now, and this is how it's going to work!"

I woke up and went to sleep with lists running in my head. I could also carry on a conversation, complete chores, serve in board meetings, work at my job, feed and discipline the children, care for pets, shop, cook, clean and more with these messages and lists running continuously at full speed, simultaneously during my tasks.

So, after much ado and trying to trust the process, I still felt like I needed an extra life raft. Heck, I also needed more paddles, life jackets, and spotters, but a life raft would have been nice. So I did the next thing I always do in times of anxiety, uncertainty and overwhelm. I picked up the phone and called my Aunt Joanne who was my hero from childhood.

Besides being my favorite aunt, she was my sitter growing up, my mentor, role-model, scout leader, and best friend. She was also a busy mother, wife, and a successful, talented entrepreneur of a wedding cake business. Looking back now, I know why I always adored her. She taught me more about life, love, grace, authenticity and honesty by watching her from the wings, just by how she was being and living her life, never lecturing or telling me how to be. She never talked about it, she just *was* the living example of how to be. Most importantly, these gifts and qualities were given to me so I could pick up the baton in life when it was being handed off.

As I grew into an adult, she was always my head cheerleader, the voice of calm and reason, with extra confidence all sprinkled into one. She was also my anchor when I just needed a quiet port to rest in, always there and ready to listen when I needed someone to hear my concerns out loud. With an astounding way of picking up my ideas and piggybacking them into more fruitful plans, I knew she would help quiet the storm.

She suggested an extra paddler and life support might be my new-found friend Sally. But, how could I ask her? After all, our comradery was over staying out of doing too much! Yes, Aunt Joanne was always my best counsel and knew just what to say. "Just ask her," she encouraged. "The worst she can say is no. After all, she has a daughter riding in this boat too!"

Sally answered the call and became my extra life raft for sure! She delivered the last bit of confidence I needed to start paddling this boat down the raging river of life. My spirits lifted when we formulated a plan and forged a new partnership to be co-leaders for troop number 145. We agreed to get our feet wet slowly and see how things went.

Each of us carved out a half day of work, twice a month, from our already burgeoning schedules. We shared the meetings in our homes every other week directly after school and planned out the first year to keep things light and simple. It would consist of a few fun trips, a couple of easy hikes, and at least one fun craft meeting a month. Yes, we both walked on eggshells with our new mantra of, "We'll see how things go," adding an additional clause of, "and we'll re-evaluate this situation at the end of each year."

We often mused about the "I told you so" implications of our first meeting. And when things got hectic (which they did on occasion) one of us would recite the narrative, "See, they can reel you in," with enough cynicism and humor to break up the stress. However, we never regretted our decision for taking action on the plans or the new bonds of friendship we were anchored in for life, while we forged ahead together into the unknown, down the raging river.

Chapter 2
BIG LESSONS IN SMALL MOMENTS

T HE ANSWERS DID not arrive quickly or easily for that matter, to set out on this new endeavor. Of course, I took some time to wrestle with my soul and gather more research, to see if I was on the right path. Nevertheless, I did not take the responsibility too seriously, and that is not to say I took it too lightly either. It was more of a delicate balance, teetering on both sides of this issue. Much like parenting, I could not be flippant about the duty, however, not so taut we couldn't have fun! That was the key word. *Fun* was what I was trying to create more of in my life, as well as within the troop. It was a graceful line to create without completely dropping the ball on either side of the net.

Our weekly meetings started with the simplest thing; everyone seated in a circle. We all took a turn checking in with the group by finishing one or more of these opening statements: The best thing about my day was _____. I was happiest when_____. I was proudest of myself when_____.

These priceless moments gave so much insight into the emerging personalities of each one of the girls. They all had different shells to break out of. What seemed insignificant and easy for some, was obviously opening new doors for others.

My daughter, Heather, and Sally's daughter, Kelcy, skated through this exercises with the same ease as the theater productions they performed in at school. Additionally, they were in the safety of their own homes with their moms running the meetings. They usually chattered away about themselves with the same comfort they had being on a stage.

However, sharing or talking openly in our circle of eight girls was a bit of a stretch for the rest of the troop. A challenge that most girls overcame with time. Except for Chelsea, for whom this ice-breaking routine just became more agonizing with time instead of improving. It was apparent that she was more than simply bashful or shy. It was actually painful to watch her struggle with speaking about herself in the group setting.

She was always smiling with sweetness oozing from ear to ear. Her dark brown eyes fluttered nervously around the circle and back to the floor avoiding eye contact. Her long, beautiful, shining, Polynesian hair wrapped like a cape around her miniature petite frame of caramel-colored skin. She was the essence of light and love.

These opening ceremonies transformed her beautiful sunshine smile into a look of worry and uneasiness. Her breathing labored and became heavier the closer it came to her turn. Staring at the floor, she pleaded with us to skip her. Only to have her wringing her hands anxiously and going through the same ritual of waiting until the end. Determined to find a solution for these uncomfortable episodes, I intervened at the beginning of a meeting and suggested, "Why don't you go first, Chelsea?"

With a little more coaxing from Sally and the girls, we finally convinced her to "try it" by doing something new. After all, the name of our Brownie badges were "Try Its" for a reason. We were always trying new things. She began with three minutes of complete silence, which probably seemed more like an eternity for her and the other girls. She finally spoke, slowly and without breathing, managing to utter several highlights from her day.

Towards the end of her share the smile that we all know and love returned to Chelsea's face. She ended with a deep breath and a sigh of relief exclaiming, "And I was the happiest and the proudest of myself when I went first in the circle just now."

Uncontrollable laughter broke the ice with the girls while I choked back the tears welling up in my eyes. I felt so much pride for her at that moment and cloaked my emotion, not wanting to make a big deal over it. Yet I knew what a huge deal it really was. Witnessing how much she grew in that tiny space of time by the twinkling in her eyes, she sat in absolute peace and calmness for the remainder of the opening with her angelic smile returning.

From that day forward, she was enrolled and hooked. All on her own, she figured out how to step up and go first. No more letting it build up and pushing through the pain. This was a moment for me to note and remember and a huge growth moment for Chelsea!

The following year, more growing pains set in for Chelsea when we announced the plans for attending our first Service Unit Camp. There would be roughly 10 troops or approximately 100 girls plus 20 leaders from our district in attendance. The camp theme was "pluralism" and we were asked to plan our activities around raising awareness about this subject.

Each troop would also prepare and perform a small skit at the campfire to educate and raise awareness about diversities and pre-judgements. We selected a skit called *The Blob* for entertaining our peers. Chelsea's fear escalated to panic almost immediately when the girls began selecting their roles.

We made cardboard cutouts of squares, circles, triangles, and stars, painting them red, orange, yellow, green, blue, and purple. The blob was, well, a blob, of white fluffy nothingness, sort of like a cloud. The girls screeched with laughter every time we rehearsed the lines, "Hi there! I'm a blob. Just a blob. Nothing but a blob. All I do is blob."

Practicing the play was more of a lesson in fortitude for me, than a rehearsal for them. By now the girls were more familiar with one another, beginning to have behaviors more like siblings than just a troop of friends. They were comfortable joking and teasing each other, along with laughing at themselves.

They also developed a big sister protective instinct over Chelsea. When the shy and timid Chelsea popped out of a box for every practice, they offered a rescue by taking over her part. She was more than eager to relinquish it over to them. "We will all support Chelsea with her lines," I reassured them, "but not by doing them for her."

With time and practice, she actually got more comfortable reciting them during a meeting. Getting her to say them in front of 100 strangers, well now that was going to be yet another performance on the stage of life.

Excitement amongst the girls grew as plans and preparations for our first big three-day camp weekend drew closer. In order to get them ready for their first overnighter in a tent at a big camp, we were required to have a "Try It" camp in my backyard. The focus was on the most entertaining and delicious aspects of camping. With the hope that Chelsea would get her feet wet with fun and dissuade her from dropping out with fear!

Our mock-up camp was a hit, practicing campfire songs, making s'mores, playing games, and earning "Try It" badges. The big favorites were making shadow animals behind a sheet with flashlights in the tent. Followed by the big brothers and dad sneaking around outside our tent making weird animal noises in order to scare us. We managed to hold our own by getting them back. We quietly gathered around the opening, unzipping the tent and waiting for them to make the next move. Everyone shrieked at the same time, spooking us all together in the end for hysterics and laughter.

My personal favorite was trying to get eight giggly excited girls to finally fall asleep after all the animation and stimulation! These were the best of times and what memories are made of. These little moments of nostalgia, traditions, simple fun, and uncontrollable laughter made the entire journey a worthwhile trip.

Two weeks later, all rested up, practiced and prepared, we marched off for another run of *Camp Giggly Girls II*. Nearly the split-second after we pitched our tents, unloaded the gear, and sat down to review the weekend itinerary, the heavens opened up pounding ten inches of rain on our campsite for the next 48 hours. Well, it seemed like ten inches anyways!

The girls hardly noticed and never skipped a beat, while Sally and I huddled under a makeshift canopy in front of the tents. In a torrential downpour, we watched them dance for hours like sugar plum fairies in rain slickers. We mused about the fact that they actually believed the rain made camping more fun because they got to use all the rain gear they packed this time, while we lamented that it was the camp from purgatory in a monsoon!

They came in and out of the rain to play their favorite games, such as the famous "three-headed, purple, people eater monster" skit. Three girls squeezed into one large rain poncho and played the role of the three-headed monster. The remaining girls sat as an audience and asked the monster dumb questions like, "What is your favorite food for breakfast?"

Each head of the monster had to answer in a split second, not knowing what the next head would say, in order to make up a complete answer or sentence. The first head blurts out "Ice Cream!" with, "Cake!" and "Broccoli!" coming from the second and third heads. And so it goes, with each girl taking a turn answering as the monster.

"Where do you live?"

"In a cave, on a desert, by the beach." "Do you like to read?"

"Yes, sometimes, no not really," while the third head looks at the other two heads, shakes her head in disgust and rolls her eyes. The silly faces alone kept Sally and me in stitches as they screamed and yelled with sidesplitting laughter for hours of silly self-entertainment.

This game was also a good warm-up exercise for the campfire skits to follow. Unfortunately, the antidote of laughter was not enough medicine for Chelsea to get through a preliminary practice, much less a performance. The grip of stage fright was taking its toll, and she sounded like a case of laryngitis was setting in.

The girls offered up their big sister love again by taking over her lines. However, I made some hot tea with honey to warm up her vocal cords. She and I practiced our deep yoga breathing together while sipping the hot concoction. Finally, she squeaked out her lines in our last rehearsal while I massaged her shoulders.

I felt Chelsea's pain almost as much as she did. Not just from the trembling transmitted from her quivering shoulders through my fingers, but on an emotional level as well. I remembered my own experience with the fear of public speaking from my high school days when I almost threw up from it, so I knew all too well how real it was for her.

Relating to her emotional and physical pain was easy and automatic. How to help her through the valley of fear? Well, that I wasn't so sure about. This was one of those "wing it" moments. I would have to trust and turn upward for the answers.

*

It was time for gathering all the troops at the campfire. The girls paraded from the tent on a high note, still offering to rescue Chelsea from her lines. All I offered Chelsea was my hand, holding it out with a smile for reassurance. She stared back silently pleading with her eyes to stay behind. And finally, with a little coaxing, we left the boundaries and safety of the tent.

She and I walked behind the other girls at a snail's pace. About half way across the campsite she pulled on my hand taking a step backward. In a tiny, frail voice she yelped, "No Miss Pat, I can't go." Sally caught the reaction we both were expecting and rushed over to help. I motioned her to go ahead with the other girls and confirmed we would be along soon. Kneeling down, I looked closely into her eyes. They were now begging me to take away this

worry and let her stay within the coziness of her old nest.

I scooped up her dainty, little hands that easily fit inside my closed grip. We both stared into one another's eyes until they were ready to spill over with emotion. I felt her heart beat racing through our clasped hands. In a low, calm voice I began speaking slowly, "Chelsea, we can do this." I paused for a quiet moment and let it sink in, then repeated, "We can do this together, Chelsea."

We stared motionlessly into each other's eyes until I felt her courage building through her breath. I repeated our mantra several times over., giving enough time for each breath to settle in and slow down the racing heartbeat.

"We can do this together. I will be right behind you, and I will be speaking with you. All we have to do right now is take some deep breaths," reassuring her that we wouldn't move until she was ready.

Practicing together, we synchronized our breaths. After all was calm and still again, I encouraged her with a smile. She reciprocated with a reluctant grin, and I knew we were ready to push forward.

"Are you with me?" I cheered her onward, bouncing our clenched hands. Telepathically, she answered me with a smile. As we shared a nod of approval, I felt the waves of confidence passing through our clasped hands. We sealed our new treaty with a hug and some renewed energy. Hand-in-hand we trekked silently towards the campfire site.

All the girls filed in a circle around the fire pit and perched on log benches. Each troop sat in their respective groups. Chelsea sat next to me still practicing our yoga breathing. We smiled quietly at each other, while all the squirming, wiggling and giggling going on in our vicinity eluded her attention. Being caught up in her own vortex of thoughts demanded a lot of concentration.

I could see her whispering lines to herself while two other troops performed before us. Upon hearing the introduction of Troop 145, I could hear her breath quickening to short sips of air. Sally motioned the girls to stand, and I knelt behind her placing my hand flat on the center of her back. I whispered our new mantra, "We are doing this together. Just take slow, deep breaths with me first."

The skit began with Heather and Kelcy, who were strong in the performing arts, taking on the lead roles. They belted out their lines with Broadway confidence, and the next few girls followed suit. Our rendition of *The Blob* was in full swing with everyone doing well and having a good time. Well, except for Chelsea of course.

On Chelsea's cue, I gently rubbed her back and whispered, "Say it with me." At first, her voice was faint and weak while we recited the words together. I kept rubbing her back to help relax her breathing, and partially to keep her standing.

After pausing in the middle of her lines, we kept it going with reminders to, "Stay with me and do your deep breaths." The next few lines she picked up speed and strength needing very little help from me. After a few more, I was barely whispering the words, and she was almost speaking alone. By the last line, she was going solo and had now grown wings, soaring off on her own.

At the conclusion of our skit, she whipped around squealing, "I did it, Miss Pat! I did it all by myself that time." Prouder than my own first experience I exclaimed, "Yes you did, Chels! Yes, you did."

We broke into a celebratory hug and sat down holding hands. I could feel her heartbeat racing, but this time from busting loose and flying. The grin lighting up her face said without words, *I got this, and I can do it again!*

Sitting quietly and smiling at Chelsea, I began thinking, *so this is what it's all about. I now see why we are all here together and why I was called to serve. It was for the common purpose of teaching and learning from each other. Just when I thought I was helping her learn and grow, she took off and pulled me up in her wings, creating a new lesson and showing me what's most important. Truly giving me the answers to "Why me? Why am I struggling here? Why do I need to make time for these girls and this troop? Why am I moving mountains in my schedule to carve out moments of time?"*

The answers all came flooding up at that moment. I was there to learn and grow *with* them. To truly understand what is really important in life. Right when I was showing compassion and lending support I received the greatest gift of all. It's in giving to others that we receive the greatest gifts in life!

CHAPTER 3
WHO CAN RESIST GIRL SCOUT COOKIES?!

I F I HAD to pick a word for Girl Scouts, and could only choose one, the defining word would have to be "cookies." I think the world would agree the word cookies is synonymous with Girl Scouts! They seem to define us! But truly the word cookies doesn't even begin explaining Girl Scouting or our troops.

Cookies are, however, the gateway to everything we do. They provide the financing vehicle for most, or at the very least, a majority of the events and experiences we share in this sisterhood club of youth.

They create revenue for community service projects, finance troop trips for experiential learning and teaches, with a small business model, our first money handling skills. Armed with these tools and programs, we practice serving locally in our communities, nationally in our country and globally for a much bigger and higher purpose. We also bond with each other while connecting and working in a national network, but, most importantly, we discover how to learn, serve others, and have fun at the same time!

In other words, it's more complicated than just cookies! However, the cookies are still the means to the end, with regards to all we learn and do. So, it all comes back around to one thing, how Girl Scouts are aptly defined and identified by the word "cookies!"

Cookie sales are a big focus for a couple of months each year, not only for our troops of course but all across the country. Getting into gear and finding a willing victim, (clearing my throat) I mean, cookie mom, was nothing short of a miracle. There should be a special corner located in heaven with comfortable seating for these selfless individuals. They are surely unique and set apart from all the rest. This person runs the engine of the troop's major funds on a short, demanding time schedule, as a volunteer, while performing all their other regular family responsibilities and life's duties, simultaneously I might add.

Then there's an entirely different species, the District Cookie Sales Coordinator Volunteer. Let's just say they will achieve sainthood during their service. They handle (in our service unit anyway) approximately 30 other troops' cookie pre-orders, booth sale scheduling and PR with retailers and troops, financial spreadsheets with numbers and balancing money for all the troops in the district, as well as running and organizing their own troop. They do this saintly act in the wee hours of the night, for the love of serving others, without any monetary compensation whatsoever, and very little help and understanding.

It was a *big deal* when a plane loaded entirely with Girl Scout cookies landed in the islands. The nightly news would cover the event and show the aircraft landing. Upon arrival, a fleet of trucks engaged for land transports to Aloha Stadium to begin the distribution process. Each troop had an appointment and a short window in which to pick up their cookies from the stadium site.

The cookie moms scheduled months in advance for each troop's bulk orders pick up. This was a well-oiled machine scheduled and planned months in advance to get the cookies out of the hot sun and into the hands of Girl Scouts across the state for deliveries. In our first year, I worked with the troop's cookie mom coordinating our schedules for pick up of our 200 or so cases. We blindly chose a pickup date and time months in advance, never knowing if it would fit into our daily lives and erratic schedules, matching the well-oiled machine when the day arrived. We simply crossed that bridge when we got to it. While standing one week in front of that bridge, helping with the pick up at the stadium wasn't fitting into our cookie mom's timetable.

She asked for my assistance to replace her. With all the moms working or home with other small siblings, I was the last go-to, safety net, backup minivan taxi driver, in a pinch, when no one else could do it, person/mom most of the time. So, of course, I was picking up the cookies for our troop in the middle of the day, in the middle of the week, between work appointments, 'cause that's how we rolled. Just get 'er done! In other words, we flew by the seat of our pants, or in short, we just winged it!

The morning of my scheduled pick-up day, my son called from the hospital. His son (and my first grandson) who was born 12 days earlier, was still in Pediatric ICU. His current condition was worsening, and he was being evaluated for possible medevacking to California for heart surgery. My son was overwhelmed with this news and in the middle of a meltdown.

I got off the phone with him and called Marilyn, our district cookie sales manager and coordinator. She and I had only spoken on the phone a couple of times and had yet to meet in person. She cheerfully took my call and rescued me by offering to collect our massive order, if I (or someone) could retrieve them from her by that evening. She would not have room to store them in her house with all her orders in the family living space. I agreed and rushed off to the hospital.

I still had client appointments scheduled for later that afternoon, with no way of reaching them in all the urgency. I also had kids to pick up after school that could not be put on hold. And all I could think about was the prayer I recited over and over, all the way to the hospital.

"God, please hold this baby in the palm of your hands, lift him up and heal his body, making him whole, well and healthy and please send me an angel right now with an extra set of wings to help me drive this car, and somehow finish all the tasks at hand today without any incidents or failures."

I was on autopilot all day for sure and worked through the list taking first things first. Somehow our prayers were answered, and my grandson, Micah, improved enough that day to prevent a trip to California. However, his severe health problems and surgeries continue to this day. I managed, on that day, to console, cry, hug, and hold hands with my son, daughter-in-law, and her mother until we could do no more but wait, pray, and trust.

I rushed home and picked up the kids from school, finished all my clients at work, and made the trek to Marilyn's house in honor of our agreement. On the late drive, I began my silent lamenting of *Why me Lord? Why me again?* The tape hardwired within my monkey brain just seemed like it took over when I was most fatigued. Once depleted, I could no longer use reason and logic to answer all my silent banter.

I continued my whining session with God all the way to my destination. "Why did you have to choose me for this job? And, why did I pick all of these things to do in my life? Why is all this happening to me? Why now? Why all at once? And lastly, I am so exhausted, why aren't you sending me an angel with more help and an extra set of wings, to help me get all of these things done?"

The weariness had taken over now, and I was on a self-focused path of lamenting, "Why me Lord? Why me?" I arrived late at the address after getting lost and becoming a little more befuddled. I was still complaining while getting out of the car and muttered to myself, "That was the worst set of directions I have ever received!" (This was still back in the day before GPS when we depended on human communication and interpretation to guide us.) I walked towards the door with frustration, fatigue, and forsakenness wondering why I was on this mission, much less the planet! *Why am I such a lost soul right now Lord? Please give me a reason or an answer to all my helpless-feeling questions.*

The woman opening the door melted my heart into a pile of liquid adoration. And there she was, my hero, Marilyn, the Service Unit Cookie Sales Manager, organizer, troop leader, mom of two, career women, rescuer, saint, and angel with an extra set of wings.

I reflexively extended my hand to introduce myself, realizing a split second too late that she could not return the gesture. From a birth defect, she had no arm on the right and only half an arm on the left, with which she was holding a phone in the two pincher fingers on that arm.

We both laughed at the error, which she had probably witnessed many times before. I reached out and gave her a hug that I probably needed more desperately at that moment than she did. She motioned towards her carport while walking in that direction, concluded the phone conversation, and introduced herself, all in route. Reaching the pile of boxes, she exclaimed, "We need to hurry with this inventory and get these boxes loaded, I have 10 more troops to contact before it gets too late." Hence the status of Sainthood for District Cookie Managers in the days before the internet. She carried and loaded boxes with one-half of an arm and two fingers as fast as I could carry two, and never skipped a beat.

I worked alongside her in awe of the grace and beauty she possessed and marveled at the strength and energy she owned and commanded to do it all with. On my drive home, I reflected about my own mother who raised four children, worked full time in my father's business and never walked a day in her life, after the age of two, without leg braces and crutches. Polio completely took her leg muscles with its crippling reprisals.

I never really thought of my mother as being handicapped or different than anyone else, and neither did she. My mother was my mother, and I was born thinking she was normal, and that's the way mothers get around. I was well into grade school before I saw that she was slightly different. But never really paid a lot of attention to details, like how she couldn't climb stairs, or get into certain places long before ADA laws opened a whole new world for people like her. She simply accepted or adjusted to her limitations and pushed the envelope whenever she could.

She never once talked about what happened to her, complained or otherwise felt sorry for herself. Because she carried on so normally, I really never connected so deeply and reflected on how she must have sometimes struggled, until that day. It hit me over the head so profoundly on the drive home. She must have felt the same way I did today, at many points in her life with more reasons to get frustrated, overwhelmed and distraught, but she never showed it.

She picked up the hand she was dealt in life and gracefully played it without whining, lamenting or otherwise asking for any special attention. She was my hero for teaching me so much about life, discipline, and how to persevere. I didn't realize until that moment how I was gradually absorbing the lesson. I was also learning the actual lesson was to be obtained through experiences and struggles to fully understand it.

How easy it is getting caught up in my own narcissistic world when I get tired, stressed or pushed to the limits. I knew intellectually that life had many parts with great highs and deep lows, and that my reactions were always a choice. However, I needed to step it up and start choosing to celebrate and embrace every minute.

I profoundly needed to learn how to make lemonade when life handed me lemons!

Yes, I turned a corner that day and made a conscious decision to serve with awareness about the bigger picture. Understanding this was all just a test in life, catapulting me to the next level and preparing me for the real important stuff, like mentoring eight young girls into leadership of self, of their families, communities, and our society.

I knew at this moment that these lessons were revealed for a specific purpose, to bring forth discernment and understanding. I also understood now, why I would need patience when they hit their walls on the journey, and to never take it personally. I could not rush them through the process, and I knew they would gracefully receive the lessons in their own time when they were supposed to. Trusting their eyes would be opened to all that life had in store for them, at the precise moments, at the perfect point in time.

Knowing that I didn't learn this stuff until I was an adult gave me some expertise to fall back on. I certainly did not learn it by someone preaching and telling me how to behave, but instead by having strong role models gracefully living the examples for me. Absolutely, this is a delicate process and a journey full of rich lessons, but who else better to guide them through it? Yes, "Why not me?" This was what I'd been prepared for, and why I received the constant messages from the beginning, screaming "Embrace it. Run with it. Grow wings and fly with it."

Silently receiving the messages on my voyage home, I spoke another prayer. "Thank you, God, for keeping my grandson close to home and helping with his health. Thank you for sending me *this* angel today, for sending me lessons and opening new doors. Thank you for reminding me of how blessed I truly am, was, and always have been, to now be mentoring and experiencing life by working with my daughter, her friends, and our troop and being so lucky serving in our community with another angel, with an extra set of wings.."

*

Who knew a bunch of boxes of cookies could be at the center of so much learning, lessons, and drama? But they were. Cookie time was always a new learning experience, full of fun, profits, commerce and friendly competition. After the girls secured and turned in preorders from friends and family members, we took up the traditional selling practice of booth sales at our local merchants. The girls managed the inventory, sales, money, change, and public relations in their first business partnership, while we parents drove, supervised, and chaperoned the process.

Of course, most or all of the troops in our state participated in this same ritual, at the exact same time. National sales rotate by state, not putting heavy demands on the cookie bakers all at the same time. However, troops from the same region do conduct sales on the same calendar. They usually hold local friendly competitions for prizes and recognitions of the most sales individually and by a troop. But for the most part, we generally functioned and helped one another in a friendly co-op of businesses, generating funds for a good cause.

The first week of our first year, I wasn't so sure my daughter Heather would be up for selling cookies on her pre-scheduled post at the local grocery store. She had fallen off the jungle gym at school a few days before and broke her wrist. After lots of tears, grief and drama in the emergency room, she selected a bright pink cast to accentuate her favorite clothes and outfits. She was barely seven years old and yet had enough fashion sense early on to coordinate her clothes and now her therapeutic prosthetics.

Her petite size yielded the appearance that she barely looked old enough to attend school, much less old enough to be wearing a uniform and selling cookies. This was a point of contention for her, creating the chip on her shoulder, which she wore throughout her school years. The stereotype also aided and abetted the sassy girl attitude she developed that she needed to prove something to the world. At this age, she was still sporting her toothless grin and two side, pink, scrunchy pigtails that looked a bit like floppy dog ears. So, overall, she was a mess of adorableness, in a sassy teensy package.

It turns out she bounced back quite quickly from all the pain and trauma and was feeling much better by the day of our booth sale. She insisted on going out to help the troops and was so excited to wear her brand new, fully decorated Brownie uniform. As usual, she selected the outfit of shorts and a vest, with accent colors of a bright pink t-shirt, socks, and hair ties setting off the entire ensemble perfectly matching the bright pink arm cast stretching from elbow to fingertips.

Dressed to the nines, we sailed off to her first official scouting fundraiser and set up a booth at our nearby grocery store. Cookie sales were going well and in full bloom when one of my friends, and a leader from a Cadette troop, arrived about mid-shift. Margo was a tall, outgoing, redhead, brimming with humor and laughter from her years of experience with the public as an airline attendant. She never met a stranger and engaged everyone she met with wit and satire. In short, she was a traveling stand-up comedian looking for a place to land.

I could hear her coming from half way across the parking lot. "Oh give me a break, you did *not* just set up a booth sale here, with teeny tiny cute little Brownies with no front teeth, wearing a pink arm cast!! Now *that* is rich!! This *is* the lamest trick in the book I have ever seen to sell cookies!! And now I've seen everything!!"

She rushes over and gives everyone a big hug, and continues with her stand-up routine, "SO, how do you expect my Cadettes to compete with this? (hands on the hips) They got nothin'!! Nothin' like this, I tell ya, to compete with teeny tiny little toothless Brownies. We're screwed getting rid of 100 cases of cookies now! We'll be bringin' 'em over here to your toothless little Brownies in pink casts to get rid of 'em now!!" She shakes her head and walks into the grocery store.

Heather, trying to read and decipher this conversation, walks over to question what is going on. "Is that lady mad at us mommy? How come she doesn't believe I broke my arm?"

I pinched her little irresistible, freckled, button nose and explained, "She thinks you're too cute, and she's just teasing mommy, 'cause she wishes she had a little cutie like you to take home and snuggle."

Heather smiled and went on about her cookie sales without a hitch. But, being the smart entrepreneur sales woman that she was, figured out cuteness and charm will take you more places in cookie sales, and she turned on her pint-sized charisma the minute Margo walked out the door.

She was standing near the door with a box of cookies in her one good arm and snuggling the second box to her chest cradled with the pink cast. Margo took one look at Heather and burst into laughter. To which Heather pulled out the big guns on Margo. She cocked her head sideways towards her shoulder, pigtails tilted catty-corner, curled out the lips and said, "I really did fall down and break my arm, I'm not kidding."

Margo broke into hysterical laughter pulling a twenty-dollar bill out of her purse and slapping it down on the table within her benevolent nature. In her wellspring of repartees, she continued with the teasing that she was famous for, "I have a hundred cases of these bloomin' things sittin' in my living room, and that stinkin' kid is too stinkin' cute! Give me two boxes of thin mints and don't you dare tell anyone about this!"

Heather was all smiles handing her change single-handedly (pun intended) and thanking her for the sale. To which Margo revved up the engines again and was off to the races, "You guys beat everything!! I'm telling you this is the lamest trick I've ever seen to sell cookies."

Scooping up her boxes and quickly shuffling to her car, she shook her finger back in our direction, clutched up into fifth gear for maximum speed and said, "She's a one-armed bandit, (pun intended) that's what she is, she could sell ice to the Eskimos she's so stinkin' cute!" And off she rode into the sunset leaving us holding our sides and uplifting our spirits in her rendition of humorous cookie sale competitions!

I also heard about it for the remainder of the year at our monthly leader service unit meetings; she would reiterate, "Those toothless little Brownies in pigtails and pink casts, yeah, that's the lamest trick in the book, and you expect our gawky Cadettes to find something to compete with that trick?!"

Our friendly leg pulling banter (or arm pulling as it were) had all but stopped and died down after two more successful cookie sale seasons. As fate would have it, Heather fell again breaking her arm just before the onset of sales. With her blaring sense of fashion, she selected a light blue cast this time, color coordinating with the new turquoise Junior uniform she was now sporting.

I, of course, was aware of the implications and was hoping I could stay under the radar without running into Margo before the cookie season ended. But in a small community beach town like Kailua where the six degrees of separation are more like three degrees, that would be like, impossible! I could hear her train a comin' like a Johnny Cash song a hummin'. And I knew she was out there and would be gunning for me.

We were perched at our first booth sale for the season in front of the grocery store, and she picked me off from behind like a sniper from the grassy knolls, "Sooooo, you thought you could hide this from me, this time, did you?! Yeaaaah, you think I'm gonna believe it was just an accident this time??" Her eyes rolling, side-splitting laughter from the girls in the galleries and she was on a roll.

"Come on, spill the beans, you have someone workin' on the inside at the hospital gettin' you access to these fake casts, don't you? Come clean, who is it??? I'll find out ya know, this is a small town, and you can't hide anything in a small town, I'll find out who it is!"

She slapped her twenty on the table without any more resistance, banter or arm pulling (pun intended) and said, "Just gimme my cookies now, and spare me the one-armed change counting trick, keep the change, and you know the drill, not a word about this to anyone!" Turning on a dime, she marched into the store with all her redheaded flare and cookies now in tow, only to return a half-hour later with a bigger smirk on her face and elbowed up to my daughter. "Now Heather, tell Miss Margo the truth, I will get you some help. Did your mommy push you off that jungle gym, or did you really fall off?"

Heather was laughing as much as we were, "No, no my mommy wasn't even there at all, the nurse had to call her." To which Margo persisted, "It's okay to tell me, Heather, I can get her some help." She was entertaining everyone in the vicinity at this point until the joke began growing wings and taking on a life of its own.

Before exiting, in true Margo style, she threw the last flaming arrow in her personal arsenal exclaiming, "Lamest trick in the book, a Junior in a baby blue arm cast? Lame, lame, lame! I'm gonna get to the bottom of this; I know she pushed you off that jungle gym Heather, and I'm gonna find a witness!!"

And the jokes continued for the remainder of my tenure, fueled with friendly fire for completely kooky comedy cookie competitions!

*

At the end of our third year of Juniors, we received a private tour along with a news press release on the USS Constellation aircraft carrier docked in Pearl Harbor. We received this honor and excursion for being the fourth highest troop cookie sales in the state.

The girls excelled in a new program whereby the public could purchase cookies for military personnel serving in the armed forces directly from our booths at local merchants. The girls tabulated and collected payment at the booth sale, and our council handled distribution to active service members throughout the world. They also collected cards and messages people wrote at the time of purchase.

The ship we toured would be delivering the cookies overseas on its next deployment, after a few days in Pearl Harbor. We arrived early on the docks that held thousands of cases of cookies. Donned in our uniforms, we were ready to be ambassadors of our state and the Girl Scout troops. After all the hoopla, photos, and news videos, we got down to the most serious business of seeing how that big floating city worked.

Several of the highlights were meeting the ship's Admiral; sitting in his seat on the bridge; looking at and learning about all the complicated sonar, radar, and gyroscopes in the vessel's helm; and scrutinizing the view while pretending we were steering at the rudder. My favorite segment was a ride on the airplane elevator from the hangar's holding deck to the top-flight deck.

Another photo-op for the newspaper took place on the flight deck with all the cases of cookies stacked behind us like a monument. A moment I will never forget on our excursion was meeting one of the plane mechanics. The airman spoke to me when he noticed I was taking a photo under the wing and in front of his aircraft with my daughter. We especially liked the name under the pilot's window which was Crawford, and the same name as Heather's TuTu's (Hawaiian for grandmother) maiden name.

The man thanked me for working with the girls and being a Girl Scout leader. Then motioning toward the wall of boxes he said, "and thanks for the Girl Scout cookies too, we love them, especially out to sea, when we get a little homesick." I walked over and shook his hand and said, "You are so welcome and thank you very much for being on this ship, serving as you do, so we have all the freedoms and safety our country affords us." We were still shaking hands and looking into each other's eyes when he said, "You are very welcome also." While letting go of his hand, he tipped his head forward, humbly bowing in respect.

Taking a step back, he shared about having a daughter near the ages of our girls whom he had not seen for nearly five months. "I know she is doing the same at home, selling her Girl Scout cookies, and these girls sure do remind me of her right now. I will be seeing her in about another month and a half." Our conversation continued a bit further on how much time he got to spend with family, or the lack thereof.

My thoughts were drifting in and out about my second oldest son who was serving in the Air Force stationed in South Korea. This was during the Gulf War, and the pilot talked a lot about the men and women he served with. How many of them couldn't find jobs and enlisted in the service just to feed and take care of their families, but were deployed without them.

We also talked a moment about military life in the islands, and how a quarter of the scout troops in our district were military families with deployed dads as well. In the days before skype and cell phones, it was a pretty big hardship for these families, and I dealt with it in the everyday lives of our scouts, friends, and clients, living next to a military base.

We ended our conversation on another note of "Thank you again for serving," both ways. This time, I was choking back the emotion in the form of gratitude. I felt the lump rising in my throat while I was squeaking out the words, "God Bless you sir, and your family, and give your daughter an extra hug from all of us soon. Please tell her how much we appreciate her letting us borrow her daddy while she is growing up and missing him."

I had to walk away from the group for a moment before the dam broke with all my thoughts accumulating at once. I had been strong over the past year, holding in my feelings about everything going on around me. Now my heart was filled to the brim, spilling over with the full impact of sentiments about it all. This man brought home the stark realities of families and the casualties of our global unrest that nested in my heart constantly. During the past year, I attended funerals with two of my closest friends burying their sons, one of whom was my son's best friend in high school.

I recalled the conversation only two weeks earlier with my son on the phone in Korea. I was worried about him serving in a dangerous place while talks of war surfaced on the news every day. I couldn't reach him for about a week with all the phones disconnected. They were moving the entire base on the Demilitarized Zone as tensions in the region escalated. He finally called, and I spoke about my fears. His reply stayed with me easing some of the pain and worries that moms can't help but have.

He simply said, "Mom, someone has to do my job, and if it's not me, it would be someone else. But I am happy, content, and glad to be where I am, learning what I can about the world and how I might affect change in it someday. And if it's my time to go, then it doesn't matter if I'm living around the corner from you or around the world. When it's my time, then it's my time; and if you believe in all the things you raised me to know and understand about spirituality and life, then I'll see you in a better place on the other side someday. So be happy for me now, knowing that you did a good job raising me. I am serving where I belong and want to be, enjoying every minute we have now." Once again, the student becomes the teacher!

I had to let it all in at that precise moment and completely feel the raw emotion of how connected we all are on this small planet. I didn't seem to have a choice. My reactions dictated the moment, and I seemed to be flying away with thoughts overwhelming me. How can humans, so intelligent a species, not understand this connection we have to one another? How can we get so blinded we forget to transpose how others are feeling just because they aren't living in our houses, neighborhoods, or countries? We are all one, connected living beings on a small planet yoked at the core. How did I convey this to my son? How am I conveying this to the girls? Will they affect the change we need in the world to have people love and care about one another unconditionally, to take proper care of the planet, and stop all the bickering?

After I let it all in and processed the feelings, I asked myself if I was doing all I could to effect change in the world. I knew in my heart that I was doing what I could on a small scale. Was this enough? Was I supposed to do more? I felt my heart lifting with the answers to keep sharing the messages in this arena for now. It told me that this is the path I am supposed to be on, because that is where I am right now, and that more answers would come with time and, much like a book or movie, the story would unfold when it's intended.

I walked back towards the group realizing these passionate feelings were stirred up while reaching out and touching the souls of saints, looking into the eyes of these tireless individuals who were working far away from home, giving to others for something greater than themselves. The same way a majority of servants do daily across the globe. People are risking their own lives to give us all a better place to live. Police, fire rescue, emergency workers, and on down the list, all the way to parents, teachers and all the people who mentor our youth.

There is so much more that is right, good and working in our world; why do we listen and make such a big deal out of the negative issues without dwelling, focusing, and celebrating the millions who do their jobs well, with pride, in service, in gratitude, in complete selfless giving? When is the world going to recognize this and stop giving the loudest mouthpiece to the smallest few who mess it up for the majority? Or when is the public going to say "enough"? Let's celebrate these unsung heroes who show up and do their jobs selflessly, sometimes sacrificing their own happiness and families to do it.

It was an emotional day for me personally, on the roller coaster of emotions while contemplating life! It was the hugest cookie delivery we'd ever attended, and the best private tour of an aircraft carrier. Overall, it was a home run in the Girl Scout world. Once again, I hugged the girls at the end of the day to say goodbye, but this time, I absolutely felt their beautiful spirits for sure, while I whispered a simple prayer of gratitude. "Thank you God, so much, for giving me the chance to serve, and for calling me to wake up when you did. I am here now, wide awake and conscious, taking them under my wing!"

*

We did some sort of community service every year with the money earned from cookie sales. The fundraised money that directly financed projects also resulted in learning about our community, state, country, and the world. By contributing the money we raised to things we found of interest and participating in projects, we grew, learned, and developed a sense of the world around us and its needs. We also managed to reward ourselves at the end for a job well done with a cookie blaster party!

In the early years, we did several service projects at the women's shelter, community food bank, senior citizen's center and the Humane Society. We participated in three Lokahi Christmas Projects and sponsored needy children at the holidays with clothes, gifts, and food items. Every year we purchased and donated needed items from the wish list of Camp Paumalu, Oahu's Girl Scout Camp on the north shore, after decorating and signing them of course. In later years, we completed a Silver Project at the camp, refurbishing the bathrooms and showers near the pool.

We participated in National Beach Clean-up day the first six years and cleaned up Aloha Stadium after the annual Aloha Run the last four years. Two years in a row the girls staffed a "Kids Vote Hawaii" booth at our local polling station, whereby children could practice and participate in voting alongside their parents, immediately seeing their results with the live election returns on television. They were greeters for the Women of Distinction dinner, a huge fundraiser for Girl Scouts, three years in a row, and marched in six local parades.

For five years, the troop sponsored a needy child in Honduras the same age as our girls. They received and sent annual photos, letters, drawings and progress reports about their lives, families, and education. We also sent money to cover school supplies, food, shelter and clothing. We were also pen pals with a Brownie troop from the Big Island for three years, and a Girl Guide troop from England the next three.

We sponsored four girls from a Wider Ops Program into our homes, from Indonesia, Hong Kong, and the Philippines. They learned all about our interests and culture through sharing food, music, clothes, photos, talking story, and taking excursions around the island. We learned about their lives, families, cultures, and the Girl Guide Programs in other countries, simultaneously by bridging friendships.

For instance, in their countries, it was a requirement during high school for them to attend some type of community service program for at least two years in order to graduate. The Girl Guide Program we sponsored them from served as a fulfillment and gave them invaluable experience traveling and making international connections. We also wrote to them for many years.

We opened new doors to the world participating in our local district Thinking Day events every year. This national celebration happens around the world in February with troops and Girl Guides to raise awareness about other cultures. We held the rather large gatherings in a school cafeteria or park. Each troop had the option of selecting a new country, representing it the way they chose at the annual gala. Occasionally the theme switched from countries to states, keeping our island girls connected with its big sister the United States.

At meetings, we studied, explored, and prepared how we wanted to represent our chosen culture. We practiced our planned performances, made or gathered distinctive items, learned new recipes and made S.W.A.Ps. Which stands for "Some What-cha-ma-call-it Affectionately Pinned on." The SWAP is traditionally pinned on a sash, vest, wristband, lanyard or something the girl chooses to wear on her travels and adventures. It is affectionately pinned on and given as a small souvenir to remember us by. We share this unique bond and tradition with girls of Girl Guide Programs from all over the world when we get together and experience traveling with them as well.

At our local events, we traveled around the world to each country or state by visiting each booth. The day began with a flag ceremony in which my Scottish husband lead the parade for many years playing the bagpipes. After each flag bearer had traveled to her country of origin flying the flag proudly, the stage performances commenced. We experienced the distinguishing cultures by observing performances like skits, songs, dances, and music within our own backyard. We ended with travel and visited each country or state at our leisure, starting with getting our Passports stamped upon entering the booth or country, then sampling new foods, trying activities and games, and, of course, collecting our SWAPs along the way.

These rich and diverse activities were the foundation and tools in which we learned, gave back, and had fun with each other. All my fond memories of Girl Scouting and its rich traditions date back in my memories all the way to the 60s. While many things have come and gone in my lifetime, few stand out more from my childhood than the experiences I shared with my favorite mentors, friends, and comrades of our Girl Scout Cookie Brigades. They will be with me until the end and have been an integral part of growing, learning, and experiencing new things in life. They are also now an integral part of my fondest adulthood memories and friendships as well.

I am officially a paid, lifetime member of the Girl Scouts of America. However, a well-known fact among Girl Scouts is that once you are a scout, you are always a scout. Whether or not you are currently paying dues or serving somewhere. Once a girl receives her pin, she has earned the privilege and the rite of passage to be called a Girl Scout for the remainder of her life.

It is a pact with yourself and others to be honest, trustworthy, helpful, serve God, protect people, animals, and the environment, leave a place better than you found it. So on it goes for the rest of your life, and it never leaves you even when you are not currently on the childhood journey or mentoring someone. The principles live on within your personal journey.

In short, the cookies are a means to an end. They provide funds to finance many experiences, but I can't stress enough how much only associating us with the word "cookies" short-changes us and doesn't even begin to explain us. Because, like the girls themselves, the word might represent us, but it *is* complicated!!

CHAPTER 4
IT'S A GIRL THANG!

GIRLS JUST WANNA have fun! It kept playing like a record in my brain over and over through the years, and I just couldn't get it out. If cookies were our defining word, then "Girls Just Wanna Have Fun" would have to be our theme song! Like the cookie thing, it's a lot more complicated than that, but what's the point if you're not having fun while living life, learning and serving others? It's entirely about the journey as much as it is the destination. Perhaps that's why I get bored and give up talking to people who think they have arrived. We never arrive. It's all about staying humble on the journey and always being open to more learning.

We took many paths to learn and have fun! The scouting program was/is rich with ideas and provides a plethora of ways to open new doors, find new experiences and create fun with friends. In other words, they have written some fun, safe guidelines for getting started on an adventure that is as unique as you want to make it. It's likened to having a party planner do all the investigating and research for you and all you have to do is step into the room and execute. Add in the support from the group at large around you, the trained staff at council, the connections globally with Girl Guide programs, and you have a recipe for learning and fun!

We were pen pals with two different Girl Scout troops over the years, with the first being a Brownie troop from the Big Island. For three years running our friendships were fostered and grown with letters, photos, and artwork exchanged once a month. It was our good fortune and privilege to meet them during our third year of Brownies when they flew over to Oahu on a troop field trip.

The other leader and I parlayed and conferenced months in advance for our meeting at the Girl Scout Council Headquarters. The headquarters were home to a charming and historical plantation-style estate, which troops often frequented for ceremonies, events, training, and other various business. The estate, sometimes referred to as the hale, meaning house in Hawaiian, was also available for appropriation in conjunction with troop events.

The atmosphere of the hale had many captivating qualities from the old hardwood floors, to the vintage fireplaces and massive antique staircase. Large picturesque windows gave way to a panoramic view of the landscape. Uniquely crafted carvings and ten-foot ceilings regarded a presence of grandeur in the stately rooms. The entrance was supported by white columns on a sturdy wooden porch wrapping around the structure, bearing plush pillows on wicker furniture, inviting visitors to find a soft place to land.

Umbrella-like canopies of shade created by banyan and monkeypod trees reach nearly every inch of the property adding to the ancient charm and appeal. The tropical gardens soothed and tantalized the senses with sweet fragrances of plumeria trees scattered amongst lush floras of red hibiscus, ginger, and anthurium. One could genuinely feel the welcoming auras surrounding the estate with mystical properties emitted from ti leaves, and splashes of heliconia and bird of paradise. The most alluring attraction on the grounds by far was the traditional tree swing dangling on the center front lawn, calling guests to come visit this serendipitous place.

We formulated and prepared a special get together with our sisters across the isles. Hoping to make it a memorable gathering of, what else, fun! First, each girl made a lei for her corresponding pen pal, and second, a picnic lunch for an afternoon reunion of linking words to girls. In our pen pal writings, we discovered that one of the girls in their troop was deaf. So, I asked one of my good friends, Miss Jolene, the sign language teacher at our school if she would teach us how to sign the Girl Scout promise and law. We learned rather quickly and were ready for communicating on the day of their arrival.

I will never forget the look on the little girl's face when our entire troop delivered the surprise greeting of signing the promise and the law to her and her troop as our aloha gift of welcome. The moment she comprehended we were speaking directly to her, she grabbed her mom around the waist as if to hang on for the ride, followed by squeals of laughter transferring to her entire essence, and animatedly slapping her mother about the torso proclaiming her excitement. She clearly understood we were conveying this message for her, and for a moment she buried her face on momma's dress, using it to dry her emotions and gratitude. Then she quickly peeked back and forth for the remainder of the exchange with a smile firmly expressing her adoration and approval.

I couldn't wait to hold this precious little soul and soak up her energy like recharging a battery with a human hugging connector. She was absolutely a delight to hug and embrace, along with her sisters on an adventure of exploration. We welcomed our visitors to the Gathering Isle of Oahu followed by hugs and flower leis for a proper island reception. After chatter, giggles and girl things, we circled up on the lawn of the estate, bringing our three-year connection to life by joining hands and singing our familiar opening Girl Scout song, "Make New Friends, But Keep The Old." The perfect gesture and apropos for beginning an afternoon of food, fun, and games, with old friends and new!

*

Our roots are anchored in celebrating and remembering Juliette Low for founding the program and leading us into scouting. We usually commemorated the week of her birth with a donation in her name to our favorite charity, confirming thanks and gratitude. We also learned something new and educated ourselves each year about the legacy and footprints in which we traced our behaviors. A special party, a peace pole dedication, and ceremony, or simply lighting a birthday cake with candles and remembering with song were some of the ways we chose to celebrate. The traditions we created were always fun and full of folklore.

One of the special ways we gathered in celebration was our annual mother/daughter tea parties. These special events were usually quaint and casual, yet we dressed up with the flare of queens for our china clinking chatter of sipping tea and trying new delicate and dainty foods. It's a girl thang perhaps, but sugar and spice we are (sometimes).

The first year of Brownies we made paper bonnets, donned with huge bows and flowers. We dressed in our Sunday best, white gloves and hats to refine the exquisite event, and we had a photo op that was utterly a sight to see. To learn something new and for a little entertainment, I invited a good friend of mine, Teresa from church, who was a professional vocalist with the Honolulu Opera. She gladly accepted our invitation for a little girl time, while raising two boys of her own. We learned a bit about her experiences as a professional vocalist, and how she decided upon her career. We also got our feet wet, experiencing opera by attempting a few vocals with her proficient lead, making memories in an afternoon of girl time with tea for us too.

Our next tea party celebration centered on a Hawaiian theme, and we all wore muumuus while gathering at the Girl Scout hale on the Saturday before Mother's Day. The girls honored their moms with handmade leis and performed a hula for some lively entertainment. We discovered at this tea party that a spoonful of laughter went down really well with our lumps of sugar, tea, and crumpets when someone began sharing an embarrassing moment from her week.

We later adopted the new custom of sharing our MEMs or Most Embarrassing Moments at all our future tea parties. We also evolved in the tradition by adding a reward for the most outlandish of these stories with a prize befitting the embarrassment. First a drumroll of clicking tea cups, then you take a bow for living through it, and finally a gift certificate to a spa, candles, a basket of tea assortments or some other soothing gift of relaxation!

We also bestowed gifts onto the poor unlucky second place winners who provided us with moments of healing laughter, by voting with applause to distinguish the categories. Once there was a story that brought down the house, filling the room with screams of laughter and OMGs. Without a vote, we all intuitively knew who the winner was. Even the runner-up walked over and placed her consolation prize in front of the first-place winner conceding, "You have earned two prizes dear, with that story!"

No, I can't. I know! I wish I could, but I can't share it with you because these enchanted moments were just for us to share. They were full of love, laughter and unexpected moments that were rare and may never be recreated. These serendipitous moments were, in a way, therapeutic sessions while dipping into our treasure troves of stories. It was a time to be ourselves and let it all go with humor.

We certainly bonded while getting to know each a little better in the process, all the while teaching our daughters that it's okay to be human, sometimes make mistakes, get embarrassed and laugh it off with friends. However, most importantly it's that we all truly need to laugh, not take our egos too seriously, and for goodness sakes, get up quickly, dust ourselves off, shake off the mistakes and get back in the game as quickly as possible! This really is a girl thang! One that needs to be practiced, shared, mentored, and certainly passed on because that's how strong women do it. That's how we roll. We don't sit around weeping, "woe is me," and crying in our tea, but once in a while, we do dress up, donning hats and bonnets, wearing gloves you see, cause we like clinking our glasses, "talking story" and laughing until we pee!

*

As much as we loved our mom time, dads needed some equal bonding time too. Sometimes dads could be our first hero in life, and they quite possibly could fix anything from a broken bike to a broken heart, or so it seemed like some days. One of the things I was most impressed with and so proud to see, was how often the dads participated in all our events. Even in the cases of divorce, the dads stayed closely involved with participation. Statically this is a huge factor towards the success of a young girl's life.

There were events and camps planned entirely centered on and around the dads and daughters. Three years running, all the girls in our troop attended daddy/daughter camp on the north shore at Camp Pamaulu. This was an annual favorite bonding time with dads giving complete focus and devotion to their girls, escaping televisions, books, newspapers, radios, phones and distractions that otherwise divided attention at home. This was also a great time for the girls to learn about relating to men, for future references.

It was a real struggle getting my husband on the bandwagon the first couple of years. I used guilt tactics or whatever else I could find in my arsenal to prime the pump, and start the traditional bonding in nature practice for them. He was a workaholic engineer who had to have everything written down. That's another book entirely, but finally, the process gelled and he took off flying with it himself. They both came home with smiles, engineering projects and stories that will last a lifetime. Those bonding moments are some of the most precious stories my daughter has of her father.

I started, planned and executed the first annual daddy/daughter sock hop in our Hui Ho'okela service unit. It was held at a local parks and recreation gym with a silly DJ who had all the corny dance moves, mixers, and party tricks up his sleeve left over from the 50s. We decorated the gymnasium with hues of pink and white. Two huge balloon arches led the way to the dance floor that looked like a fairytale of floating streamers emerging from the revolving mirrored globe as the centerpiece.

An old fashion soda fountain, drive-in style food and theater style popcorn machine festooned the lobby. The old-time photo booth was set up inside the gym for fun. With professional dad and daughter photos taken in a mockup studio by the lobby for souvenir record magnets to remember their magical night, all inclusive.

The disc jockey orchestrated involvement with line dancing, limbo, the Macarena, a conga line and more, saving the Cinderella dance last, for obvious reasons. Everyone had to remove their shoes at the beginning of the sock hop to enter the gym. However, on the last dance, baskets loaded with one shoe from each girl were passed around the gym. Dads had to choose a shoe from the baskets and dance with the corresponding girl to the shoe of his choice.

Now if the dad was really on top of his game, he could recognize and find his own daughter's shoe. But the funniest part was seeing how many dads didn't even have a clue what their daughter's shoes looked like, much less a prayer of finding one to them. Of course, the Cinderella game ended up becoming the second to the last dance because the very last dance was understood and unspoken, it was reserved for daddy's little girl. Yes, any man can be a father, but it takes a real man to be a daddy, and real daddies go to sock hops and save the last dance for her!

*

Yes, girls just wanna have fun! And don't we all? More and more studies are revealing how important this fact and phenomenon truly is, and how it's linked to our health and well-being. Obviously, our entire physique is linked to this fact, and depression, the opposite of having fun, is not good for our health or society. So the statement or the fact that we just wanna have fun isn't just a flippant comment, it's actually a necessity of human function. So, fun was our middle name!

Girl Fun Scouts on an adventure was our mantra, and we explored all the sites of our island home like a fish takes to water. Living in Hawaii created unique experiences for certain. In so many ways, we were lucky seeing and experiencing things other girls only read about and dream of. However, in other ways, we were sheltered and isolated with an island lifestyle. We always made the best of this double-edged sword, and it never phased the girls one bit, nor did it slow them down. We did the whole shebang, from the arts to the outdoors and everything in between.

We toured the white house at Washington Place and met with the governor and his wife for photo ops. We explored Bishop Museum several times, covering Hawaiian heritage, history, and the planetarium, also going back to the traveling exhibits like the dinosaurs, and hands-on events for science day. We also took the science tour at Windward Community College, exploring the planetarium and learning about past and future space travel. We enjoyed a private tour of the Contemporary Art Museum in Tantalus, creating our own art projects in a class with a professional artist upon conclusion.

We met and worked with four book authors learning everything from, how to start a manuscript, writing and illustrating a book, to how their ideas came about and were created. These authors graciously read us their books, signed copies afterward, and inspired us to read, write and dream.

We toured the number one rock radio station during the "Drive at Five" show and talked on air with the hilarious DJs. While introducing ourselves, Heather mentioned our dog's name was Tako, (pronounced taco, and Japanese for octopus) and how it was the same name as one of the DJs. The other three jockeys never let him off the hook. They rolled with that joke the whole time we were interviewed, along with their antics about being held hostage, by a bunch of Girl Scouts wielding cookies.

During the holidays, we always attended a ballet or a live theater. Twice at the ballet in the historical downtown Hawaii Theater, and two productions at Diamond Head Theater, meeting all the actors and actresses for parties at the end.

We took the movie tour exploring Jurassic Valley at Kualoa Ranch. The devastation from bombings in the most recent film *Pearl Harbor* was extremely visible. We walked in the humungous Godzilla footprints and posed for photos on the famous log spot from the *Jurassic Park* movie. At the end of our tour, we watched the making of a commercial with trucks digging their way up a hillside at a scary ninety-degree incline, looking like they would flip over backward. Don't try this out, without professional stunt drivers! Then, going back to the ranch on two more occasions for horseback riding.

We trekked all over the botanical gardens at Waimea Falls Park, watched cliff divers, played ancient Hawaiian games and joined the dancers, shaking our booties to the drums of Polynesia. We made several excursion trips to the ice skating rink, one of which we took lessons from a professional Olympic trainer, who was also one of our book authors.

We made our annual pilgrimage five years in a row to the University of Hawaii on girls' sports day, broadening our interests in sports while meeting and working with the Waihene's (Hawaiian word for women's) Sports Stars. On these trips each girl played at least three sports of her choice in a rotation of events, spreading our wings and trying new things, with semi-professional athletes.

Adding up all the stats during Daisies, Brownies, and Juniors we did twenty-two sleepovers at homes and sixteen nature hikes. From this point on the list, I realized there was a theme developing with the numbers, and I kept hearing the tune from the "Twelve Days of Christmas" while writing it out. It was just funny that I couldn't get the tune out of my head, so I had to try it out, (since "Try Its" are the name of our Brownie Badges) and it got funnier when I sang it. Go ahead, try reading it without the tune popping into your head.

We did… eight Service Unit camps, seven pool parties, six thinking day events, five movie trips, four pizza parties, three Service Unit picnics, two pen pal troops and a tour on one aircraft carrier.

Ha-ha! To say the least, we were busy little bees, having a bunch of fun!

In these first three levels of scouting, each girl earned and received a Daisy pin, Brownie pin, set of Brownie wings, Girl Scout pin, World Girl Guides pin, leadership pin, Program Aide patch, three Bridge badges, seven stars for seven years of service and membership, six Aloha Ambassador patches, six Honor Troop pins and charms, twenty-four try-its and twenty-six badges.

In the tradition of saving the best for the last, we did just that with our famous cookie blaster parties. They were the best! We saved them for last, for a very good reason. They were our reward and the celebration of a job well done. This was how we brought our year to a close, with a blast of fun, in a celebration! It was also a time for reflecting and thinking about doing it all over again, next year, of course, after we rested up, were fresh and ready to go on another big adventure!

It's hard to put a finger on any one of our excursions or events to say which one is or was the best. Surely, if I polled the girls, a different answer would pop up for each. I, however, encompassed all of them like a new day dawning, with awe and gratefulness. Mostly seeing the girls all giggly and excited was the highlight and pinnacle for me. Everything after that was just icing on the cake.

We worked up slowly doing cookie blaster parties and built up some momentum with time. The first year we started off with the Discovery Zone, a virtual padded room full of crazy bouncing off the walls with ropes, climbing towers, nets, labyrinths and ball cages.

The next year it was a little lower key with putt-putt golf, a video game arcade and a pizza party at Bay View Golf Course, graduating the next year to The Ultra Zone for ultimate laser tag at its best.

We traveled back to Hawaiian Waters Adventure Park two years in a row because we couldn't get enough of the waves, waterfalls and slides the first time around. Moving right along, the next year was some cultural fun at John Hirakawa's Magic Show in Waikiki, with a night of food, entertainment, and illusions Vegas style.

A real crowd pleaser was the trip on Dream Cruises with a barbeque lunch, trampolines, diving boards, slides and snorkeling on a catamaran, all-inclusive day of fun in the sun, off Waikiki Beach.

However, the year we Dozed with Dolphins, sleeping all night next to the tanks at Sealife Park, was clearly the highpoint trip for me. I will never forget waking to view these magnificent creatures angelically floating in their habitat and watching them attentively through the glass, experiencing eye contact as if they could feel into my soul while simultaneously watching the sun rise through the tranquil ocean in a brilliant ball of orange fire. Also, catching site of the girls peacefully scattered around the aquarium tanks with pillows, blankets, stuffed animals and sleeping bags, I knew immediately witnessing this scene, that our world was all right, and I was all right with our world.

These moments carved out in time will never be taken away, with the memories etched in our consciousness forever. I now have riches beyond the tangible things that will only fade with time, and the treasures I have gained knowing and experiencing these girls growing up can never be replaced. They have healed all the things in the world that I could never explain, with their love, laughter, and excitement, through their exploration, learning, fun, and games.

Looking back on all the experiences, growth and fun times, I can easily see why I was so concerned, frightened and overwhelmed about taking on this daunting task. Also, reflecting back on all the experiences, growth and fun times, I *can't* see why I was so concerned, frightened and overwhelmed about taking on such a daunting task. Here it is again, the proverbial double edged sword that I am now eternally grateful for, and thank you God I heard the messages and picked up the baton.

Observing in the rear-view mirror lends a keener vision of depth, abundance, and fertility about these gifts and lessons. Considering all the contributions to my life, every challenge on the journey made the trip all worth my while.

During this time, I earned and received an Outstanding Leader of the Year award and pin. Up until my name was called at our annual leader's appreciation dinner, I never knew the accolade existed. They are rarely given out, so not unusual that I'd never seen or heard of this award. I wasn't just speechless; I was completely taken aback. I learned it is a very prestigious national honor of which very few are given, except to a person going above and beyond for their troop and others.

Who was this person standing at a podium receiving all this praise? In the beginning, I doubted myself, thinking I could not do the job, much less handle taking on such a task and several years later I'm receiving this acclaim. Letting it all in and receiving praise, I learned was a lesson in and of itself.

It took me some time to truly be okay with this award and actually feel like I was letting in the praise. I felt somewhat uncomfortable and overwhelmed about receiving it. But why? All I needed to say was thank you. Why all the weird feelings? Intellectually, I thought I knew about self-esteem, loving myself, confidence, and being a strong woman, but now being tested on these values, gave me a whole new perspective. What was causing so much discomfort about owning this praise? Why couldn't I identify with it? Did I honestly not feel worthy of praise?

Feeling worthy was only a part of it. Growing up, I was taught to be humble and not boastful about myself. I began thinking, where is the line between humility and accepting and acknowledging one's own greatness? Women and girls often receive mixed messages and negative labels if they are assertive, confident and selfassured. Whether we want to admit it or not, there is still a double standard when it comes to women being strong and assertive.

Because my mother couldn't walk or drive, I was partially raised by my grandmother who lived with us and was born in 1902. She spoke to me about marching for women's rights to vote at the turn of the century. She also passed on some of the double standards from that period which still exist today. My grandmother was a strong lady who was out in the forefront championing for women's rights over a century ago. However, I saw her labeled negatively my whole life, which got handed down today unfortunately in the double standard I still see, feel and hear in our society.

Women who are outspoken, stand for something, take on leadership roles and become passionate or proactive in the wake of a cause are still labeled today. I agree, if there's assertiveness without politeness, courtesy, and kindness, it needs to be addressed. However, even when these manners are engaged, there is still a pervasive overtone that women are pushy, brash, brazen, lippy, domineering, controlling, nagging and don't even get me started on the "B" word.

It's not just men brandishing these labels either. I've heard more women do it than men. Perhaps because it's so politically incorrect nowadays, for men to even think in these terms. I also feel women impose this double standard on one another when their own insecurities show up. I've witnessed women wielding their insecure behaviors at a time of jealousy, feeling less than, or when they felt the need to be in control of something or someone.

There is nothing wrong with being assertive, confident, selfassured and proud of it! However, when we do these things without love, kindness, care, and politeness, we get into trouble, and herein lies the slippery slope. In other words, if we are doing all the things on the responsible list of effective behavior, we shouldn't hear any of these labels again, right? Quite to the contrary, as I stated above, they simply rear their ugly heads in other forms.

We know when it is present, and we can feel it even when it's unspoken. Its omnipresence is invading women's dignity in our society and increasing at an alarming pace. This whole convoluted mess of detrimental mixed messages and labels gets tossed around in our world without ever taking the time to consider and look at how much these actions, feelings, and behaviors are affecting us. Much like pounding a nail into a board and pulling it out, there is still a hole left in the soul of a person who feels these invasive thoughts.

In other words, it's a mess out there, and *we need* to clean it up. We *need* to celebrate each other! We *need* to celebrate ourselves! We *need* to step into our own greatness with boldness, confidence, and certainty and own it, with humility and graciousness, each and every one of us! We *need* to stop being afraid to own it because we might get labeled if we do so.

When I say "own it," I'm not talking about the glammed up acronym list for the "B" word here either. Because no matter how many times you put positive words after each letter of the "B" word, you still have the Webster's definition starring you in the face. We're not fooling anybody here, and we all know it still means the "B" word. I'm talking about stopping the use of that word. Stop using it for yourself and saying you're proud of it. Stop teaching it to our daughters. Just stop!

Be kind, loving, positive, caring, confident, humble, and polite to yourself and others, and step into your greatness! Own it with positive affirmations and kind words, because that *is* the difference between confidence and insecurity. It makes the difference between intellectually knowing about self-esteem, owning it, and actually feeling secure. I know that I know this because I had to learn by walking through the fire to get it. I had to do my homework. I had to sit with myself and examine where I fall short in all these areas and more. I had to step up to the plate and accept my award, own my greatness, love myself while experiencing and feeling the difference between intellectualizing it and owning it.

Why was it so important to know, experience and feel these things? Because, if I'm going to pass them on to eight little girls watching from the wings, then I better start being the essence of an outstanding leader; loving myself, stepping into my greatness with no apologies, and feeling and owning my own self-esteem.

While I was encouraging, supporting and trying to build up the girls and their self-esteem, I truly had forgotten how to put myself on the list. Being proud, strong and humble along with extending kindness to myself, was another lesson I was learning with on-thejob training. It was a huge lesson which I indeed was in need of learning in order to pass on the baton because it's not all *just* about giving to the world and others. We women folk forget, as natural born nurturers, it's also about giving to ourselves, and recognizing how and when to do so. It's about being a strong woman, mom, and mentor without losing yourself in the process. It's about passing on the torch with love, grace, and ease. It's about all the stuff we talk about but struggle to put into our works. It's all about a girl thang and what we *do* with our quirks!

Chapter 5
A TIME HONORED TRADITION

 **W**E DECIDED TO hold our Brownie graduation at the Girl Scout Hale for a memorable experience. The hale would lend ambiance and dignity to this momentous occasion. It may be so cliché to say, but it's the only phrase that truly fits here, the time went by so fast, and now it's time for little Brownies to bridge over to become Junior Scouts. Or, as we say in scouting, becoming a lifetime Girl Scout. We celebrated all the achievements in the traditional fashion by gathering with families and hosting a sit-down dinner for our ever -famous Brownie Bridging Ceremony.

Families arrived as usual on infrequent time schedules allowing for social interaction and free play for the girls and their siblings. These were the best of times for romping, running and fooling around. It was very therapeutic watching them yell, scream, and let loose with such abandon and incredible spontaneity. As if it healed my past and gave me back a childhood by retracing it through their frolic, I savored these precious dashes while wandering into unrestricted thoughts. Like when did the line get drawn ending all my innocence and propelling me into adulthood? I don't really recall how it happened because there was no specific day or event, it just happened slowly over time. Sometimes I could float a thousand miles away searching for a reason. Possibly going beyond reason, into fantasizing about a place where we never had to grow up. Why can't we keep our simplicity and sparkle forever? There must be a place like this; I just know it.

This time of relaxation and drifting were my favorite aspects of the journey and, in my opinion, the most important offerings unto ourselves. Rendering a halt to these elements of our gatherings were the most difficult for me to transition. However, back to the real world of keeping time agreements and schedules, we must go. For this task, I brought my rainbow-colored sphere made of parachute material, adding a little organized fun as the precursor to our graduation ceremony.

Gathering everyone on the front lawn, including parents, we encircled the massive wheel of kaleidoscope colors. With everyone gripping the edges and suspending the colossal orb, I tossed several beach balls on top. We shook, rolled, whipped and swirled the balls around on the parachute like waves into a storm of variegated colors. After we had shaken all the wiggles out of even the smallest sibling, we went for the mushroom finish.

On the count of three, we all raised arms at the same time, whipping the parachute over our heads running underneath it and pulling it behind us; sitting down quickly on the edges, in a wind tunnel cave of majestic hues in a circle overhead, laughing, giggling and smiling at each other as I announced, "And, let the ceremonies begin!" I led the group out from under the parachute and across the lawn, like the pied piper, into the hale.

The large sun room was set up in theater style chairs for families and parents, with a bridge in front as the stage. Each girl lit a candle and placed it on the accolade table in commemoration and honor of her light and contribution to the troop. We began with a prayer giving thanks and gratitude for all the auspicious moments we had shared together and asked for blessings on the ones we were about to embark.

The girls lined the stage to the left of the bridge wearing a new Junior vest or sash of their choosing. Sally and I stood on the right side with badges, pins, and patches lined on the candle-lit table behind us. Moms and dads arrived at the front stage by our side, one at a time on their daughter's turn of bridging up. After the scout crossed over the bridge, her dad strategically hugged her around the waist, turning his daughter upside down.

This eccentric maneuver was fun, as well as a tad amusing. It also had its moments with unpredictability, but who better than a dad to pull off this whimsical feat. To be strong enough, hanging onto them for dear life, yet caring enough to be gentle and basically not hurt them. Luckily this auspicious ritual arrives at this age. One more year of growth and dads might not be lifting them off the ground for this transition of life.

Yes, this post was mostly for dads, unless of course, the dad had to be away for business, which was the case for my daughter, Heather, then big brothers will do, and my oldest son Andrew showed up for duty to pinch hit for Dad.

Sally and I took turns pinning the girls with their official clover leaf USA Girl Scout pins. The pin was placed on their sash or vest right side up while the girl was suspended upside down. When the dad (or surrogate dad) turned her right side up, the pin remained on the uniform upside down.

In order for the girl to turn the pin right side up, she must perform or turn a good deed, and for the rest of her life, she is an official Girl Scout honoring the pledges and promises of scouting, by landing on her feet and doing or turning good deeds for others.

My son Andy had the easiest task by far, with his sister's slightest silhouette, coupled with his youth and strength vying in his favor. However, his 6'7" stature added comic relief, and logistical complications next to, and for Sally's 5'2" frame. Heather was yelling, "Oh my gosh" when he scooped her up in liftoff from the ground.

While I traded places with Sally, who couldn't reach Heather's sash for pinning, Andy decided to swiftly take the matter into his own hands (literally) and fix the problem himself. With a loose grip, he let her torso slide through his grasp, clamping a hold on her knees at just the right moment, and placing her at the perfect height level. She was squealing again and giggled, "What if he drops me on my head?"

To which Andy simply replied, "It's okay Heather, she already did that to me when I was a baby, you'll be fine." What a piece of work, right out of the mouths of babes! I, on the other hand, maneuvered this priceless adulating moment without tears, distracted by their antics and side humor.

These paramount moments stand out and have stayed with me the most during their scouting journey. Probably because it's when I noticed them change the most, from little girls to becoming young ladies. They were beginning to understand the world in a more complex way, with some of their innocence being left behind. Is this how the line gets drawn? It just happens with age, wisdom, and understanding. It's what we as parents want for our children. For them to be normal, experiencing new things, growing up, and eventually flying away from the nest, but when it happens, it's so bittersweet.

With my daughter being the last of four, I was constantly wishing I could slow down time to savor every minuscule moment. It's peculiar how this process seems to be in slow motion for the first child and feels like it moves at lightning speed for the last. I can't even begin to comprehend, or relate to, what it would be like with only one child. Perhaps a more mixed bag of emotions for sure!

We concluded this memorable and inspiring commencement ritual with a formal dinner befitting the occasion, including all the fine touches of white linens, china, and crystal. Bestowing them with gifts, hugs, and leis in true Hawaiian style, and the after party was just as exhilarating as the beginning. We all finished strong, yet ready for our summer retreats! It was always fun to get together, celebrate and support one another, and just as rewarding to unwind, relax and reflect on all we had accomplished, learned and were grateful for. This extended family was truly united and building bonds for life.

Heather and I recounted the day's events while she was all tucked under the covers for our usual bedside chat. Her dad was the only parent to miss this prominent and pivotal moment, but she never complained about his noticeable absence. She had grown accustomed now to his work coming before family obligations. I felt bad for him having to travel for work, but more so, I felt worse for her.

She reminisced about how much fun it was being turned upside down by her big brother, and with her familiar deep throaty giggle, she added some regret, "I am glad Andy was there, but I still wished Dada had been there too, to help Andy turn me upside down."

I pinched her dainty freckled nose changing the subject, more for my sake than hers, "Well, Andy didn't need any help getting you off the ground little lady." She giggled again, then broke into laughter, "Yeah, but he almost dropped me on my head, that was sooooooo funny!" We both giggled and laughed moving on in conversation about the evening's highlights and events.

"I'm a real Girl Scout now," she beamed, clenching her hands into a fist, and shivering her whole body with excitement! "And I know what I'm going to do for my good deed." We both giggled together with her enthusiasm while she continued, "I'm going to have a tea party for Margie under the Banyan tree with Amy and Natasha to tell her how much we love her and that she is our good friend."

Amy and Natasha were her two best friends living on our street, and Margie was an elderly lady that lived across the street. Margie was always making things for my kids and joking with them while they were growing up. She loved cats and rescued every stray in the hood. At three years old, Heather pitched a fit getting her dad to give in on his no cat policy, allowing us to adopt one into our home. From then on, Margie was especially fond of Heather, taking her in under one of her wings.

I reached over, embracing Heather, trying to get out the words, but they seemed to be caught with the lump in my throat. I could not have been more proud of her than I was at that moment. I knew then that she was going to be alright. Everything I had done with her up until that moment was guiding her in the right direction. She was getting it now and with one of the hugest points of life, to love and serve others. She was growing up so fast and time was slipping through my fingers, but with that thought, I drew comfort in knowing that someday she would become a great woman, leader, mother, and friend. For now, she was a gift, as well as a gifted person.

I held her for a few moments while still on the edge, choking back the tears I'd been holding onto since the graduation ceremony. I managed to tell her what a great idea she had, and how we could start planning it together in the morning, adding, "I am so proud of you Heather, and I'm so glad you picked me to be your mommy." She looked at me kind of funny asking, "I picked you?"

"Yes, I think you picked me, 'cause before babies are with their moms, they are watched by the angels until they pick their moms, and then the moms take over for the angels until the little angels grow their own wings." We both laughed and kissed good night, with thoughts of angels watching in the wings. Tucking her in quickly, I retreated to the living room.

I desperately needed quiet time with some hot tea and honey. For very different reasons than four years earlier when I ran to retreat in my comfy meditation chair, escaping from feelings of overwhelm. This time on an extraordinary high point of being overwhelmed with the cup running over! Spilling out with love from every pore, I realized every minute up to and including that moment was so worth the price of admission. Hearing her understand the meaning of life at such a young age and echo it back, made this journey so worth the rally.

*

The evening was bursting with reflections, not just in looking back at the evening's graduation ceremony, but beyond to traditions as far back as my memory would serve. How far I had traveled since my Brownie years. I could still see my old green faded uniform of light cotton cloth and could recall feeling the same excitement as my daughter when I received that shiny gold pin. Feeling pride when I turned it right side up on my uniform, not in just moving the pin, but in remembering what it felt like to turn a good deed.

That feeling has never left me, and I was made profoundly aware of it by the same ritual we performed with my daughter and our troop that evening. It changed my world for the better, understanding that I needed to be kind, caring, and considerate of others and our world. This is what passing the torch feels like. I couldn't wait to call my Aunt Joanne, to share stories and photos with her. This was our bonding time, remembering a coming of age story, and a rite of passage. Every year on Mother's Day I sent Aunt Joanne a card enclosed with photos of our troop events, and many years later my cousin gave me the scrapbook upon her passing, where she kept them all intact.

In reflecting and looking at recent years, it was just a trickle of time, and yet it seemed like we had traveled eons in those few short years. I recognized how much we had grown together and had fun along the way. How could I have struggled with the decision earlier on, to be more involved in her life? How could I be more pleased with where we are now? What's in store for us now? What's next? It was always like Christmas morning wondering what's just around the corner.

This was also a time to look ahead and think about new peaks. Time for more dreams, creating and moving into the future.

Change could be easy, wonderful, and good or difficult, bad and hard. It could also be needed or unwelcomed, but one thing was for certain, it is always ever present and inevitable. Moving forward on this constant river of life was ever present and alive.

All my reflections about my daughter, my family, the girls, life and the ever-present changes were truly a part of the journey. My reactions about everything always became clearer in my journaling. I had to journal about everything it seemed, for my sanity, or to keep it all in check. Not really sure, or perhaps it was beyond my comprehension, like a divine appointment, but it was a compulsion for sure.

It felt surreal like I was watching a movie about my life and I was just the actress in it, playing my part. I don't know if this was the coping mechanism to slow down the process and stay present in the moments or something more evolved to create the works I am now producing?

But journaling did help me take into account the needs, the moods, emotional states and mindsets of others, as well as my own. There was so much going on dealing with parents, young girls, other leaders, public relations and the local council. Everyone had opinions, viewpoints, feelings, concerns sensitivities, passions, ideas, and beliefs all associated with this mission, and again with my own thoughts and emotions on the list.

I found meditating also helped calm my mind. I could even meditate while doing the simplest chores like cleaning or gardening. This was when my mind went to complete peacefulness. It was perhaps when I did some of my best work. Rather than getting into a comfortable seated position and dozing off, I could relax from the calculating lists running non-stop in my brain by doing a simple, mindless, rote task. Thus, hearing my inner voice directing me, I always came up with the best ideas when cleaning something.

It's as if this is when God is speaking to me the most, and I can hear the messages the clearest. I found peace and solace while quietly using my hands for something that was a no-brainer. Now when

I hear the passage 'cleanliness is next to Godliness,' it brings up a whole new meaning for me. I also had one of the cleanest houses in the hood, despite the four kids and all their friends running amuck, using and abusing it.

I had tons of support around me from the council to the parents. Sally was always the ever-present backbone of our troop, full of ideas, resources and ready as a sounding board. I always had my mom and Aunt Joanne to fall back on during our much-appreciated conference calls for sharing, brainstorming, and support when I felt overwhelmed, but journaling helped me put everything into perspective. After I talked it out with all these wise women, meditated and listened to God, then I wrote it down.

All of these modalities helped with setting me up for listening when the girls explained what it would take, and what was necessary, for them to stay in and continue with scouting. They were all on the fence about signing up for the next level and committing to Juniors for three more years when we brought it up the first time in a meeting.

Later in the year through a round circle pow-wow discussion, they explained their apprehension, "We're all good with the fun stuff, and games, we like the learning parts okay, and trying new things", but they made it abundantly clear they weren't signing up for the very same program if they stayed in another three years. They wanted some changes, and they wanted to be in charge of deciding what they would be doing.

They were definitely growing up, becoming more opinionated and thinking for themselves, and I loved the spirited negotiations that followed after laying the ground work. We had this discussion well before graduation day, getting a pulse of where the girls were aiming to go. The questions on the table were simple, yet complex in their depth, requiring that I mostly listen and only clarify what I didn't understand.

I truly needed to listen, and not only hear but understand what their needs were, in order to develop and help them to the next level. Now my role would be gently supporting and safely guiding them to their ambitions and next goal. Easier said than done, but this is how the discussion went. Do you want to continue as a Girl Scout? Do you want to stay together as a troop? Are you having fun? Are you learning useful things about yourself, your community and the world? What are you interested in and what are your passions? What are your dreams?

We discovered six of the eight girls wanted to continue and stay together for sure. There were a few changes and some conditions they wanted to have a voice in. Their requests were very simple and took a little bargaining to finalize the agreement.

We talked it out, wrote it out and massaged the new plan, taking into consideration everyone's needs and input. The discussions led with the majority wanting to focus on the outdoors for our future. They expressed interest in earning a hiking badge for sure, maybe an environment badge, and quite possibly work up to an outdoor survival badge at some point.

This got the creative juices flowing for most or all of the girls. With the exception of Kelcy, who started grimacing with the mere mention of the words hiking and outdoor survival. These were not her forte, and I knew we were treading on thin ice with her for sure. We had to find and include some of her strong suits to keep her involved. Striking the balance was key in order to have everyone on an even keel.

We parleyed a list of everyone's interests and ideas keeping with the group's synergy. I added the fine arts like theater or perhaps the art museum, hoping to peak some of Kelcy's passions. She was in a gifted art program at school where only a select few were chosen to attend. This is where her gifts lay and needed to be fostered, somewhere intertwined in this unwelcomed territory of the great outdoors. She certainly perked up and showed some interest when we landed on this avenue.

Everyone loved sports day at the University of Hawaii and camping at Pamaulu, so those easily made the list. Some new interest in science was tabled and added by Tanya and Heather. Also, some interaction with animals spiked the debate, and there were no dissention votes in this arena. We escalated our conversing with perhaps a community service project involving the humane society. Lastly for fun, we added horseback riding, pool parties, ice skating and movies to top off the list.

At the end of our treaty talks, they all held out for what I called the big three. It was no more, walking in parades, doing community service at the senior citizens center and cookie booth sales. To which I countered with, "We cut back on booth sales to one booth per girl, per year, and we try to step it up in the presales, and the parades and Senior Center can go." They all smiled, ratified with a vote, and we had ourselves a deal!

The plan was set in motion, and we were excited and ready, forging ahead into some brave new adventures for three more years. This time with the girls sitting up front and beginning to steer the vessel down the proverbial raging river of life and these girls were way more certain and self-assured than I ever was at their ages.

I was pleased with our collaborations and communicating the plans. It felt like I was now on their ride with my own lessons in life yet to be unwrapped. With the biggest lesson revealing itself, already under my belt, to trust my instincts more and stay out of my head. This was another, "easier said than done" cliché with life's circumstances usually dictating at every turn.

*

My husband's frequent flyer miles account now sat at 90,000 with no end in sight for his work travel, and I was looking at going it solo for a great deal of the ride.

Sally was stepping away from the co-leader position to focus her attention on her aging mother-in-law with dementia. She would still be helping with troop activities and would stay one of our greatest supporters, but not taking on any more leader trainings, meetings, camp trips, and full-time responsibilities. In mastering lesson number one, I finally learned to relax and trust these challenges by simply waiting for the next door to be opened when one door was closed, waiting with trust, grace, and patience for everything I needed to present itself.

I did the usual planning, prep, catch up work and sending up prayers over the summer, with a wild house full of kids, and no time to focus on what I didn't have in place. As fate would have it, relief was waiting in the fall at our first monthly leader's meeting. Another leader, Kathy, found herself in a similar situation flying solo with a troop of six girls. We discussed our troop dynamics and agreed to a Brady Bunch marriage of joining girls and resources using our troop number.

All of the girls in our original troop were entering fourth grade at this point, with the same for a majority of her girls. This was a tumultuous age for most of the girls, and they didn't like themselves all of the time, much less us pushing them to do anything. I had to dance carefully around their delicate egos and temperamental mood swings. Keeping them involved and having fun was like walking a tightrope and challenging, to say the least.

We focused on our outdoor theme and took up some easy hikes to get started. Mostly trails that were paved, level, short and exposed us to walking long distances as a group. We also accomplished all our goals earning badges in the arts, theater, sciences, hiking and adding on a tour and service project at the humane society. We skated through the first year on a prayer and a promise with our new friends, and the expertise and help of the new leader, Kathy.

By the end of that year, Kathy's daughter was losing interest in scouting and getting busier with other activities, especially sports. Over the summer break, Kathy and her daughter decided to step back from scouting, looking into different adventures, and I was back to square one looking for reinforcements. All roads seemed to lead back here, so no need for full blown panic mode this time. Getting into trust mode was a constant theme, waiting for the next door to open, and I actually got more adept with lots of practice. I was just guessing at the time, but this must be what growth looks like, learning to have trust and waiting with patience.

The second year of Juniors was getting off to a slow start, and I was really to blame this time! Well, indirectly of course. We can also blame it on life's circumstances dictating everything! Our Service Unit Manager, Patty, who was the sweetest, most amazing woman I ever had the pleasure of meeting, had just resigned due to a military move. Her husband Ken, also an amazing man and a lifetime member of scouting, a huge support to her and the service unit, was retiring from over 20 years of military service, relocating to the mainland.

Yes, Patty was the head cook, and bottle washer of our local district called the Hui Ho'okela Service Unit, with approximately 25 troops in membership. In English, Hui means group and Ho'okela means of excellence. Our group of excellence had just lost its momma bear, who was the glue, the energy and the life of our troops. She was our go-to advisor, special person, and the nucleus, meeting with all of our leaders monthly. She kept us organized, informed, trained and otherwise functioning as troops.

The service unit was truly at a loss! Patty and Ken were a remarkable duo of leadership, now off on a new adventure. They needed replacing and were sorely missed. The Council District Manager, Jackie, also a dear and extraordinary woman, searched the coffers and stockpiles all summer for Patty's replacement, no stone unturned, she could not find a willing participant or victim to take on this arduous position.

It was a full-time job managing all the troops and events in our district. It also entailed finding chairpersons and overseeing about a dozen committees, planning and implementing all the annual events happening in our service unit (or local district) of troops for the year.

It would require coordinating, scheduling and setting up recruitments in schools at the startup of the school year, developing and creating new troops with girls and leaders, and handling any changes during the year if girls and leaders arrived or left. With a third of the troops in our unit on or near a military base, the latter was a full-time job in and of itself.

Then add in the small details, like troubleshooting and communicating with all the troop leaders while being a liaison between troops and council, overseeing massive amounts of paperwork required for liability getting done correctly, handled on time and filed properly, oh yah, and lastly, set up, hold and officiate monthly meetings with the leaders. Oh, when, you ask? In your spare time. Of course! After conducting her own troop meetings. Ergo, Patty and Ken were saints and sorely missed!

I know what you're thinking, by reading thus far… she did *not* take on that job!

Well yes, yours truly did! Only until they could find and train some other masochistic person to do it. With massive amounts of begging, arm twisting, not so many bribes, and tons of flattery, I said flatly, "no" at least four times when Jackie called begging, bribing with lunch, and pleading for just a few minutes of bargaining time.

Again, one of those when you're called, stand up, stop looking around for someone else, just listen and do it, moments I never regretted, after lots of prayerful moments and soul searching of course.

To say I was in over my head was an understatement. I was not only looking for a life raft now, heck, this time I was looking for a whole new boat. This river was now at flash flood level, stage three, and it was raging through life carrying me with it! I really didn't know which end was up starting our first meeting with the girls in our second year of Juniors, but now my middle name was Trust, and I was winging it for sure!

CHAPTER 6
NO TRAIL LEFT BEHIND

 I 'M SURE ANYONE could guess what my husband and Miss Sally might have said when I broke the news about the additions to my schedule, but first they announced, "I'm speechless!" Followed by hysterical laughter. However, they had a lot to say!

I learned to listen from their point of view. Really, I didn't need to respond, or even feel a need anymore; they were right. What more could I say?

I finally learned to silently and graciously accept the challenges life was handing me. I remembered the philosophy my good friend and mentor Bruce shared with me about our purpose, or the meaning of life, and what he learned from his mentor. It was simply that we are all here to learn something, and that something is different for each and every one of us. Basically, the sooner we learn it, the less we will be challenged or tested on it (paraphrasing of course).

The way I had it figured, I would learn what it was my soul needed to learn later when the lesson revealed itself. With that, I finally made a clear decision for myself, to get out of resistance, get out of my own way, and let's get 'er done! I wanted to learn whatever it was that I had to learn, and learn it a little quicker now! Easier, quieter, and less painful would be nice!

I actually learned how to relax faster and easier within this new mindset. I wasn't sure if this was how life worked for everyone else, or who had all the answers. I just knew I started to take things as they came, one day at a time without the inner turmoil and struggles. One could argue this is simply growing up, maturing with age, and happens naturally. I would suggest that we each have our own thought process and interpretations of everything we encounter. We don't all arrive at the same conclusions, level of maturity or turn out the same. Therefore, who knows what the meaning, lessons or conclusions are, or are supposed to be?

I simply knew there *had* to be a bigger point within all of this, and life, than just taking up space, air, and food. I most certainly ascertained the point of view that it was easier accepting what is, rather than resisting what isn't all the time, which left me more time and energy to focus on what was right in front of me, right now!

I left behind unnecessary worrying about how I was going to do it all, be it all, or the ever-famous, "What's coming next?" It opened the doors to a whole new world, called *being in the moment.* I was finally enjoying the *now* of life, and yoga breathing with each moment, by moment, by moment, through all the ins, the outs, and the changes.

It actually freed me up so much that I was capable of doing twice the amount of work, in shorter periods of time. Getting rid of the extra worry and doubts about myself allowed copious amounts of room for the productive thoughts and energy to occupy the vacated spaces. Sort of like the expression, getting rid of all the tenants in my head, who were not paying rent.

I needed every cell *now*, firing, functioning and humming in harmony, to manage the projects right in front of me. I knew this was my lesson for now, and it was preparing me for something else.

I could feel it in my bones; there was something I had to be ready for, an atonement of sorts. Furthermore, I knew the answer was surrendering to each event and moment now, and I had to simply wait for the why to reveal itself with time.

The majority of the girls wanted to earn a hiking badge, so that was first on the agenda. It's what we started out focusing on in Juniors while mixing with the other interests. We had completed nine hikes in the first two years of Juniors, using the K.I.S.S. method of keeping it short & simple, to get us off the ground running. We were building friendships, training, and bonding while on these nature hikes. Kelcy was even enjoying these eco-walks and had adjusted quite well with the simple ones so far. The litmus test was coming soon, and it was time for testing their skills further. We would be taking it up a notch, by adding more elevation, as well as challenges with the start of the third year.

Before I held the first meeting with our troop, I cannon-balled into the waters over my head with the first Service Unit meeting for the Leaders. It was at this gathering that the doors flew open, and an angel soared in, offering her time and talents to a troop of girls as a P.A. aka Program Aide. Her name was Crystal, and she was a Senior Scout with lots of personality, jubilance, energy and experience.

Jackie, our Council Director, brought her to the meeting to speak with the leaders about offering her services and skills of mentoring with a younger troop of girls. She was also looking at earning accolades and achievements of her own in Girl Scouting during the process. Ergo, the teaching, learning, and mentoring process being handed over. I thought she would be trampled in the stampede before I reached her after the meeting ended. I was trying to play it cool, not looking too needy by staying back until everyone else had a chance to meet with her first.

Well, that didn't work out so well, I just broke down and begged, "please choose me, please choose me, please!" We both laughed at my desperation and I gave her my phone number and meeting times. She would visit our girls and check out all the troop dynamics along with all the other offers she received that night.

After our first meeting of introducing Crystal to the girls, I received a phone call that she was interested in mentoring our troop. She explained that she would be a good fit for the girls because she "kinda" understood where they were at on their scouting journey. I was so relieved to hear this, because I didn't have a clue how to help them, especially at this complacent age.

She explained about quitting scouts for a short time at their age and could relate to the feelings, behaviors, and attitudes they were currently experiencing. Apparently, I was so far out of the generation gap that I had forgotten how to relate. She further explained how sometimes peer pressure dictates that scouting is "uncool or nerdy." I certainly did relate to that statement, and as much as things change, things stay the same. That was on the top of the hit parade list of why I quit early. However, this is where I didn't have a clue how to help them and only knew that I needed help.

So, what is cool at their age? How do I make it cool? Can I make it cool? These and many more questions inquiring minds have asked for the ages, in the parent/teen generational gap of adolescences. She also went on to explain that with a little time and maturity, she grew more confident and independent, by using the skills she gained before leaving and realized how much she missed it. Fortunately, arriving at the decision to return before graduating.

She was literally a *Godsend,* and we were a match made in heaven. Crystal was the glue at this time that literally held us together. She was the miracle and missing piece of the puzzle I had to trust from the beginning. The intuitive voice I heard during meditation was giving me the answers from the start, "I will give you what you need when you need it."

Yes, Crystal was my saving grace, and I am truly indebted to her, even to this day. She was and is a shining example of how the scouting program works and how we pass the baton from one woman to the next, lifting one another up in growth, love, and life. The scouting program was designed and developed with this in mind, for the older girls to help and do the mentoring with the younger ones. Filling in the gaps, buying us time, until the foundation cures, takes root, and they are ready to spread their wings and fly off on their own.

Crystal was the perfect role model for them. She had energy and ideas that I didn't. She could talk and express herself on their level, and the girls liked talking with her. In other words, she wasn't an adult yet. Most importantly, she wasn't un-cool like their nerdy leader and moms, who just weren't getting it. It was their theme song, "Parents Just Don't Understand!" Better yet she understood their mood swings and emotions having just gone through them only a few years earlier herself.

Yes, we truly scored with this articulate Punahou High School student. She picked up the slack, bridged the gap, and got these young girls motivated again, something I wasn't quite adept at figuring out on my own, especially coupled with all my new assignments and responsibilities. In so many ways this delightful young lady saved our troop from falling through the cracks.

They all gravitated to her naturally, while she helped them see what was possible in their futures, not just as scouts, but as young women. The girls were often using phrases and quotes such as, "Crystal said this, Crystal said that" or "when Crystal did this," and my personal favorite, "Crystal doesn't do it that way, she does it this way."

They were like little mini-me sponges looking up to her, and they wanted to be like her when they grew up. They wanted to be her now. She was so poised and graceful, pulling it all off with elegance and dignity. This is such a tribute to her mom, her scout leaders, and the scouting programs in which she was learning, teaching and modeling how to be an appropriate sister to other girls.

I adapted our meetings and schedule, to include Crystal with as many troop activities as possible. Our first challenging hike to start out the year would be up to the pillboxes in Lanikai. However, I needed to establish some new ground rules, mantras, and positive affirmations. The girls were coming up with a lot of negative, self-defeating, whining and complaining behaviors at this awkward tween stage of life now. It's when they're not really old enough to be unsupervised, yet they're becoming more adept, competent and feeling their oats. In short, they actually thought they knew it all, and it was quite comical watching them tell me so, on many occasions. After all, we were raising them to become strong leaders, and they were simply stretching their wings.

My daughter Heather was actually the master at this charming behavior earning her the affectionate nickname Miss Bossy Nickers, bestowed upon her by TuTu (Hawaiian for grandmother). We were all amused by the endearing pet name from my Scottish motherin-law and her namesake. However, we learned not to use it with any frequency when she became sensitive to this lovable phrase. My daughter was simply flexing her wings, and cleverly mimicking what she constantly witnessed her momma bird doing. She simply needed a little more time with flying lessons to perfect her delivery.

All the girls were beginning to act out and feeling just as impervious with their communication issues. Besides the strong attitudes, we had what I called the *I can't do it* syndrome. It was constant and the theme that wore me down the most. They were standing on the cusp of childhood and young adulthood and couldn't get a foothold on either side of the crevasse. It was time to address some of these growing pains.

I came across a story in the book *Chicken Soup for the Soul*, in which a school teacher was experiencing the same behaviors with her students. I loved the way she taught them, by leading them to take a profound look at their thoughts, words, and actions. I decided to take a page from her book (literally), implementing the idea on our first hike. I followed her lead having the girls write down all the things they could not do on a single sheet of paper.

We got quite in-depth with this exercise, "include *everything* you can't do, on your list," I cheered them on with additional encouragement from Crystal. "I can't get my irritating brother to leave me alone," Heather wrote down. "I can't do math," Danica wrote. "I can't climb that stupid hill in Lanikai," Kelcy wrote. They were on a roll after we primed the pump with a few hot topics to think about. "I can't think of anything to write down," Chelsea chimed in.

"There ya go, write that down, I don't have any ideas, I can't think of anything to write, I can't do this exercise." She laughed at me like I was the court jester, going mad. We coaxed them until the lists were bursting with all the things they couldn't do. I can't run very fast, I can't stand green beans, I can't get an A on my spelling test, I can't get Aja to like me, I can't win at playing basketball.

Once we had a full compilation of their lists, we folded them up, stuffed them in backpacks, and set out for our hike. "What are we going to do with these lists, why did you want us to write all that stuff down?" Everyone inquired over and over on our travels. "You will see soon, let's just get on our hike first."

They all looked at me like I'd just grown two heads. I could only imagine the thoughts they were conjuring up in their creative little brains about how crazy, kooky and weird their leader was right now. Although I couldn't help but muse all the way to our destination, I had to keep my poker face on, like this was all very normal.

Upon reaching the trailhead we gathered for a brief talk about safety, and then took turns ascending the steep, narrow incline at the beginning of our footpath. Chelsea and Heather jumped out in front, ready to excel in their element of a physical challenge. Crystal took the lead keeping up with them out in front. My husband also attended this hike and flagged the girls staying in the middle section. I brought up the rear making sure the girls at the end were safe and holding a good pace with the group.

Taking the first look at the steep slope, Kelcy stepped back, pointed to the trailhead and said, "You want me, to climb up there?" To which all kinds of amusing thoughts came to mind. I wasn't laughing at her, or unsympathetic, I was simply watching her grow, flap her wings and flutter a bit. It was hard not to smile in such a manner that didn't allow her room to hover for a tad in practice. So I went with, "I know it looks a little overwhelming Kelcy, but we are going to take this just one step at a time, you and me together, I'll let you go first."

She jumped on the trail, rolling her eyes and thanking me with a note of sarcasm in the reply. To which I simply answered "you're welcome," following quickly behind her. After initially musing to myself, my thoughts wondered whether either one of us was going to enjoy this expedition.

About thirty feet up the first rise, she stopped and said, "I don't think I can do this Miss Pat. Can we go back down now?"

"I know it feels like your overwhelmed and uncomfortable right now, so let's stop, take a minute to rest, get a drink of water, and then we'll walk a little more, one step at a time, right?" She looked at me with nuances of desertion, like "You've got to be kidding me, lady, you think a drink of water and a rest is going to make this mountain go away?" I pretended not to notice and kept praising her on how well she was doing.

My internal thoughts with Kelcy were the ones I wrestled with the most. She was the one, merely holding up the mirror for me to take a look at myself. I was more the "Just buck up, and power through it" type when it came to physical challenges. She was my reminder to balance it out, and practice using sensitivity, kindness, and understanding for those who weren't created exactly like me. Yes, I had the most to learn from Kelcy, and she would prove to be a prodigious teacher.

She gave me some of my best classroom experience on this hike, and I profoundly learned that being patient, empathetic and supportive is truly the fastest way to the top of a mountain. She and

I were aptly paired for these lessons on a playing field where neither of us was employing our strongest gifts. We paused often, I encouraged repeatedly, and we made some huge gains on this proverbial foothill of life, as well as the hike.

At about the half way point on a break, she pointed up saying, "That's where we have to climb to, all the way up there?" So, I tried getting her to enjoy the view, hoping to get her mind off the foreboding presence of the climb, and suggested, "Let's not think about that for a minute. Look at this awesome view, check it out". To which she reiterated "Yeah, I see it. Now can we go back down?"

I knew this wasn't going to be easy; momma never promised me a rose garden, but give a leader a break I thought while I wrestled with my forbearance and discipline. What do I need to do? Am I doing the right things? I needed constant reminders, and I kept repeating, "patience is a virtue," as my mantra.

With tons more encouragement and lots of hand holding we pushed ahead. While I contemplated about how much was too much in pushing the girls a little further, to grow a little more on each of our journeys and adventures. I finally decided that if it came to tears, that would be our turning around point. Not just any old tears mind you. Heather, and sometimes Kelcy, could turn on the waterworks at the drop of a hat with their acting experience. I had to discern genuine fear from the drama on a continual case-by-case basis.

Kelcy was definitely uncomfortable and hitting her wall on this groundbreaking hike, but I was so proud of the way she was busting through it. Encouragement went a long way with her, as it does with most people, but it could take Kelcy from a delicate little flower to being tough as nails in one breath. She had a tenacity that she didn't even know existed, untapped, unused and undiscovered stored within her depth.

With frequent stops and using every encouraging phrase I knew, we were making great time and progress until she tripped and fell, scraping her knee, about three-quarters of the way to the top. I was right behind her nearly breaking the fall and catching her at my feet. I felt an overtone like she wanted to break into tears, but more disgusted than hurt she moaned, dusted herself off and stomped away.

I caught up quickly to check her over and asked her to sit on a rock with me for a rest while we looked at the knee. The skin wasn't open to the point of digging out the first aid kit. It was just roughed up and red, possibly with a bit of soreness ahead. I also wanted to be sure she was calm and steady before climbing again and give her more kudos about how well she was doing.

While doing our assessment, we also discovered she broke a nail while breaking the fall. To which I started joking with her, "Oh no, we can't go on, Kelcy broke a nail, *now* we have to go back down, we can't continue on like this, with a broken nail, oh dear, all this way, to just turn around, and go back down, all because we broke a nail, what a waste." I finally got a giggle out of her, and we lightened up the mood.

We cleaned up the nail and talked for a few more minutes about how close we were to the top. Seeing the finish line and taking the last pause gave us the momentum we needed for a safe launch and the final sprint to the top. The others were roaming around exploring, and inquired the second we planted a foot at the pinnacle, "What took you guys so long?"

I winked towards Kelcy and replied, "Kelcy broke a nail on the trail, and we had to stop for a little mani-pedi time. It was a little iffy there for a while, we almost had to turn around, but we made it." She laughed again and said, "Ha-ha, you're so funny, Miss Pat." She and I finally squared off on this common ground of humor, which managed to get us through this arduous and confronting task. I believe we also found a renewed respect and leniency for one another's shortcomings while ultimately accepting the lessons and messages we were both there to exchange.

Reaching the top was quite the relief, and we all supped in the views. All three hundred and sixty degrees of it. The turquoise ocean sprawled over the curved horizon with the two mokes (tiny islands) dotting the canvas on one side. The Enchanted Lakes behind us lined with homes, parks and a golf course in a bowl-shaped crater. And the Koolau Mountain Range reaching from the tip of the north shore at Mokolele Point to the geographic turns of China-man's Hat. There were blue skies as far as the eye could see disappearing into the mountain and ocean landscapes creating a postcard in four dimensions.

This was a mountain top moment and a turning point for most of us, including me. I picked this spot for continuing our "I Can't" writing exercise to drive home the point that with a lot of intention and a little effort, we could climb a mountain, get over our bad selves and do or be anything we wanted to.

They were all sitting on an old concrete bunker left behind by the military from WWII constructed as a lookout post. Staring around at the scenery and listening to me explain our next phase of the journaling task. "So, are you wondering why we all wrote out the 'I Can't' list this morning?" to which there were several replies.

"Well, glad you asked," I continued. "We are going to dig a hole, bury the lists, find some rocks to cover the gravesite, and we will commence with the eulogy after we have completed the burial service."

A few hands went up, and the rest just blurted out questions, "Why do you want us to bury the papers, what is a *ug-la-gy* and who's gonna dig the hole?" After getting everyone's attention, I explained all the finer details of the who and what and revealed the why would be explained at our funeral proceedings.

Each girl was charged with finding several good-sized rocks while my husband dug the hole. Once our tasks were complete, we all gathered around the hole holding our lists. Each girl took a turn reading her list before retiring them one by one into the hole. I read the very profound wording of the eulogy the teacher wrote in her story while the girls filled the cavity with dirt.

Her rendition was basically along these lines:

"We are all very sad today, gathered to remember our friend, 'I Can't,' who has passed away! We know how much she will be missed, never to be seen or heard from again, but she is survived by her sisters, "I Can, I Will, and I'm Going to Right Away.' We recount all the ways 'I Can't' was a part of our daily lives (with an in-depth list of the ways inserted here), but now we have to pick up our shovels, and our lives, looking forward from this day without 'I Can't.'"

After adding closing sentiments, I asked them to gather back at the fallout shelters for a snack and a recap about our ritual. They all seemed to be reflecting on the silent march for the bunkers. Once everyone settled in, we talked about the implications of not having "I Can't" in our lives any longer.

They were still young, fragile, and tiny human beings yet so strong, courageous, and full of life all at the same time. I watched the wheels turning in their heads when the expressions caught up with their thoughts in our developing discussion. They interjected with thoughts and ideas that I would never have thought of.

"Does this mean I have to say those other things instead of 'I can't' now, Miss Pat?"

"That's exactly what that means. Cause we just buried all of those things you can't do, all gone, done, kaput, finished, all we have left are those other possibilities now."

"Well, what happens if we say 'I can't' accidently, then what?"

"You probably won't, but if you do, you'll catch yourself and remember, oh ya, I can, or I will, or I am going to right away, because why?" They all yelled back, "Cause 'I can't' is dead, that's why."

We marched down the hill that day with a new-found certainty, and even Kelcy was hard to keep up with. They all sprawled out on the grass by the car and stared up towards the mountain peaks at rest. I watched them gazing at the sky, wondering if they would remember this day much after they were grown. I was also hoping it would have a lasting and profound effect on their approach to life's challenges ahead.

One thing did change for certain after that day; we didn't hear the "c-word" used, and if it was accidently remembered, it was quickly laid to rest!

CHAPTER 7

SHE'S A HAPPY CAMPER

ONE OF OUR favorite things to do was go camping, so a lot of it we did! The Girl Scout Council of Hawaii owned and operated a campground located on the north shore of Oahu, which sits about three miles up on a wooded ridge with 135 acres of prime mountain view property, named Camp Paumalu. This was one of our favorite places to camp and get away, approximately an hour's drive from my home.

We had the great pleasure and privilege of attending at least two camps a year at Paumalu, if not more. One particular trip stands out the most, during our Junior years, as a huge growth spurt and learning experience for us all, leaders included. It was a Junior Troop camp weekend open to all the troops from around the state to attend. Our Hui (or district) had five troops of girls attending this particular weekend, with approximately forty-five girls and ten leaders and/or parent chaperones.

Our troop packed up in two minivans early on a Friday

afternoon and caravanned to the mountain ridges via the north shore route. The very minute we pulled out of my driveway, the girls began with a plethora of incessant questions. Most of which they already knew the answers to as experienced Junior Scouts. So my brain automatically shifted to the obvious question of, why are they asking so many questions? Is it boredom, over excitement, anticipation, or perhaps just a need to stay connected? Perhaps they were checking to see if I was still awake driving? My brain just couldn't seem to get off "what is it?"

Around every winding curve of the ocean view shoreline, they billowed yet another question.

"How long is it going to take us to get there Miss Pat? Can I open my snack and eat it on the way to camp? Do we have to help with making the food or setting up the tables tonight? Are we sleeping in the A-frames, the cabins or the chicken coops this time? Can we stay up late tonight if we don't make any noise? Are we doing skits tonight or tomorrow? Or both nights? Do we have to pick a buddy at camp this time? Can we make s'mores both nights? Are we hiking this weekend? What are we having for dinner tonight? Can we go in the pool as soon as we get there? Can we do the three-headed purple people-eater monster as a skit? Do I have to take a shower before I get into the pool if I don't want to? Why do I have to take a shower if I'm going to just get wet in the pool anyway?"

At first, I tried to figure it out, second I tried to ignore it, and then after fifteen minutes and another twenty inquiries around every scenic snaking curvature of the shoreline, I decided to address it. I'd heard women use three times the amount of words to express themselves as men. If this is most certainly true, based on the list above, I calculated that my head was going to explode before we reached the turnoff for the three-mile climb to the summit grounds. I made a quick executive decision to table *all* questions in the car until we reached the camp to address them all at one time!

I began gingerly, not wanting to discourage conversation during the drive, but still addressing the need for curtailing the Q & A session for a more appropriate time. "Girls, let's have a new rule in the car. Let's save all the questions for and about camp until we arrive at the camp; we can talk story if you like, share whatever you want to talk about, even listen to some music, but no more questions about camp for the rest of the drive, please, so Miss Pat can concentrate on the driving. Can you help me out with that?"

The response snapped back immediately from the second row by my daughter Heather who was never shy or afraid of challenging (nor offending) our fearless leader, me. She was quick-witted as well as assertive, retorting, "Isn't that a question, and why can't we ask questions?" It seemed to be an unwritten rule for the leader's daughter to take up the charge with the inalienable right of questioning authority for the troop – a role my daughter was all too happy about fulfilling, as if there's an unspoken responsibility or duty passed along to her for grilling the leader when the troops are unhappy. I often wondered if the girls gave her a look to get her started up, or if she came up with this protocol all on her own. Nevertheless, I was all too crafty than to be pulled in with her banter.

"Why, Heather, you are right, so clever of you to notice that was a question, so let's let that be the last question until we reach the camp while we relax and enjoy the ride." It usually took a firm, kindhearted reminder to get her off the high horse of correcting me and to change the subject completely. However, it never meant she'd stay off it for very long; it was simply a reprieve for brief intervals, in which she'd saddle up soon and often at this age, contesting me at each turn and intersection.

The new car rule became a test of wills, in and of itself, and they couldn't seem to help themselves reverting back to uncertainties within minutes after invoking the new rule. So, I finally developed a new response, which only annoyed them in the beginning, and didn't seem to slow them down for the long haul. As they absent-mindedly blurted out inquiries, I answered back with the question, "Is that a question?" To which they quickly copped an attitude and retorted, "Why can't we ask questions?" Every time! To which I replied every time with, "Is *that* a question? I thought we covered the 'why' when we established the rule?"

We played this game all the way to camp, which never seemed to faze them, and wore me out before the weekend ever started. I was ecstatic to see the camp parking lot knowing I could escape this fuselage for a breather and a much-needed stretch break. I could already feel it creaking into my bones while trying to use my best poker face and appear completely relaxed and calm. Jumping out of the driver's seat, I asked if anyone needed to go to the bathroom before we unloaded the gear. To which the entire posse shouted back at me, "Is *that* a question?" Relaying their best mocking tone of their audacious leader revealing they undoubtedly needed a break also!

"Okay girls, you got me, everyone take a few minutes to freshen up. I'm going to take a stretch while you use the bathroom. Please bring one of the loading carts on your way back from the break, and we'll all meet for check in by the dining hall in about 15 minutes." While the girls pulled gear out of the van and took turns making bathroom runs, I walked over and parlayed with a few leaders standing near their cars.

My opening line was clearly talking smack but also designed to blow off a bit of steam. "Now I know why half the leaders quit after Brownies and the troop numbers fall off so drastically." Without waiting for a response, I continued to answer my not-so-subtle opening, "because they can't take the bazillion questions, and their brains implode" which erupted into therapeutic laughter and started our very own little "cheese and whine" fest about how we were all experiencing the same thing.

"My brain feels like spaghetti," I started up with the whine therapy again, explaining the drive up with about a zillion questions and how I tried to address them. The floodgates of lamenting opened, and we were off to the races talking about this awkward stage of life that was taking its toll. We were giggling like a bunch of school girls about the tween behaviors when the girls returned to ask, what else but a question. "Where are we supposed to take our gear?" They droned while we all burst into screams of laughter. Not *at* them mind you, although it seemed so, but because it seemed so much like a punch line to all our banter!

I answered them politely but in their mode of communication, in the form of a question, "So where do we always meet and put our gear, what did I tell you to do with your gear before we left the car, were you listening?" They just stared at me like I was the three-headed purple monster, shook their heads, and walked away grunting, "I thought we weren't supposed to ask a question? That was three questions? How come you get to ask questions, and we don't?"

The leaders and I exchanged glances and few more chuckles when Suzanne, one of the leaders, exclaimed, "Boy, oh boy, we're gettin' off to a great start here."

"No, that's girl, oh girl," I countered and, "It's going to be a girl thang this weekend, hide and watch," heading back to my car to retrieve my gear.

Without another question, the girls loaded up all their gear and wheeled it to the usual meeting location in the dining hall next to the parking lot. This wasn't their first rodeo, so the deer in the headlights looks and "Where are we supposed to go, what are we supposed to be doing," behaviors were a bit over the top, even for their tween ages. They already knew the answers without the need for redundant instructions and more endless streams of questions. The attitudes and resistance were, however, a bit unusual even for them while the tension and frustrations were brewing on both sides of the street for sure.

All the troops met in the main dining hall, finished our famous and customary paperwork checks, and received printed instructions from the camp coordinators. After all the registration procedures had been checked off, we marched to the flagpole site for the open-ing commencements and where the official startup of camp took place. The traditional ceremony consisted of flag raisings, reciting the Girl Scout Promise and Law, a blessing and one or two famil-iar songs. The eldest girls always led the formal procedures assisted by the younger girls taking turns with various roles, ceremoni-ously being dismissed under and through a human bridge of arms towards our campsites.

Once the flags were raised, pledges made, and the camp was officially opened, we were officially ready to go have fun! It was "G-time" for "Going," and going is what we did best! While we were in perpetual motion "Go-time" we also did the other "Big 3 G's" like "Girl-time, Games, and Giggling!" Those happened to be what we were experts at!

However, "G-time" could also stand for any gambit of other things representing Girl Scouting, like "Grilling, Gathering, and Gallivanting" at these "Gregarious Green Getaways," which we were famous for! Say that three times real fast. We played around with tongue twisters "Galore" while "Goofing off" in our "Great Groups of Growing" with fun new experiences.

Another way we practiced having fun was the silly tradition of making-up and choosing camp names to use all weekend while temporarily discarding our real formal names. This imaginative cus-tom dates back for as long as I can remember and is up to an indi-vidual's own selection. The whimsical names, besides being unique, might bring you out of your shell, express your inner personality, or show your humorous side. So, the point was to totally have fun with it. If that wasn't your cup of tea, then you could go with some-thing completely off the wall and get outrageous with it. However, you decided, and we went with it, totally your call, pick a name, any name, and you can even burn it on a wood chip to wear as a name tag so everyone can remember it. These zany practices span the bridges of time and are part of the distinctive way we endearingly bonded during these youthful experiences.

The camp name I actually picked and burned on a wood chip was Trish, from the fond memories of my dad calling me this nickname as a child. However, the girls having no association or connection wouldn't have it, choosing another name they felt more befitting to me. The process usually didn't work this way, but they got such a kick out of choosing a name, the name for me, I finally gave up and went with it. It started when my husband chose the name Hannibal as his camp name at his first dad/daughter camp in the Brownie years, which happened to be an endearing nickname his employees tagged him with many years earlier.

Being accustomed to calling him Hannibal first, they decided I must be Clarice to go with Hannibal. To the girls, that name was more fitting, and funnier in the wake of my husband's outlandish name. It turns out it was actually funnier when they tried to say "Claaaaaricccccce" using the long drawn out phrase the way Hannibal did in the movie.

Now, none of the girls had ever seen the move, as they were certainly too young to do so; however, hearing the adults mocking the name using the mystical overtones and drawn out syllables usually got them howling with laughter. This being the point of camp using humor and laughter to build friendships, I naturally couldn't resist their parroting the silly gestures, and using mimicry with their tiny vocals to boot. Well, it was hilarious when they did it!

We had some amusing names indeed beginning with some of the camp directors, like Too Cool, Lady Hawk, Henry, and Mama Bear. Our very own Program Aide Crystal was Thumbelina, and her famous sidekick and troop sister was Pico, aka Sarah. These two young ladies were the heroes of our Hui, and the girls hung onto them like flies on sticky tape. Even as adults they still are occasionally called by their camp names robotically when we remember them with fondness.

Our bizarre camp names lightened the moods, got us away from taking ourselves too seriously, and created bonds while partaking in having fun. Well, most of the time it did anyway, after all, it's a "girl thang," remember, with all our quirks! If there was an occasional hold out still in the world of seriousness, we usually shifted moods quickly with incantations of these silly camp aliases. Such as the way the girls sang "Clarice," with their endearing humming sounds adding a high pitch tone at the end. They absolutely knew how to work it, and work it they did, especially when they wanted to talk me into doing something completely comical.

*

It was time for choosing bunk houses, cots, and receiving last minute instructions with campsite chores lists and picking activity times. After these final few tasks, it was time for the real fun to kick-in!

Each Hui or district was assigned a vicinity to set up camp in and was also free to create their own activities and schedules around the main events of the larger collective. We would meet with the other troops at various intervals for craft activities, hikes, campfire skits, and dinner in the main dining hall. The pool schedule rotated by camp sections, and we were pretty much on our own for breakfast and lunch within our Hui Districts.

Our district was one of the larger showings at this camp, which facilitated our assigned camp area to be one we affectionately called the "chicken coops." This area was located closest to the main kitchen facilities, and in camping terms, this meant indoor plumbing. It also meant a short walk to the main activities, which was as far out in the woods as I generally wanted to get at this point in time.

Camping was not really my thing as an adult, although I have fond memories of it as a child. However, the girls really loved it, while my adult body much preferred the comforts of home now. Camp Paumalu provided the best of both worlds, meeting all of our needs and goals, usually making us happy campers. I could tru-lyrelate with Kelcy, I mean Minnie Mouse (go figure!), regarding the outdoor survival theme the girls adopted after bridging up to Juniors. It certainly didn't float my boat either. There was still a pro-verbial bridge to cross ahead where we might have to negotiate the terms of an outdoor survival badge.

The upper campsites were smaller with quite a hike to reach and no plumbing nearby! Yes, we definitely scored with the chicken coop in my book, which was aptly named for their long wooden boxy structures, low ceilings, wooden floors, and half-walled screens, for open air windows. Each bunk house held approximately eight metal spring cots with vinyl mattress pads for the simple dis-infecting procedures upon arrival and departure. Throwing a sleep-ing bag and pillow on top was made easy for a quick cozy camp setup. Hooks around the rooms provided access for the rest of the gear aiding and abetting the organization of the bunk houses. How-ever, there was no setup and system too simple in which our girls could not complicate! There it was, that girl thingy thing again! I smiled A LOT!

The dining area was centrally located in our camping area on a concrete slab with a tin-roofed structure, supported by thick beams running through the center of the open-aired lodge. A rustic stone fireplace walled in one end of the structure, and two more wooden walls enclosed the space just enough to break the wind. The two long continuous rows of picnic tables butted end to end, sprawling the length of the thirty-foot bungalow. Closets at one end housed brooms and cleaning supplies, opposite the recycling bins. Just out-side the framework a makeshift sink and grill pit with more tables brought all the comforts of home into the great outdoors.

During the walk to our campsite, the other leaders and I dis-cussed the possibilities and implications of perhaps implementing my recent car rule during camp to curtail the hordes of questions still firing all around us at an alarming rate. The effort could get the girls thinking for themselves and give us a much-needed break from relentlessly repeating ourselves. We were constantly interrupted throughout the discussion on the short amble to our campsite with dozens of repetitive questions, bagging the decision shortly after the subject came up. "Let's do it, let's put the rule in place as soon as we get all the setup details out of the way" I suggested, and we were halfway to, "Camp Think For Yourself " please!

As soon as we dropped our gear in the new digs, the girls were running around like fireflies, buzzing questions about all their girl stuff. The leaders and I stepped back watching the bustle like standing under an insect light show on a dark summer's eve. The final clinch pin of humor came rushing in delivered compliments of Sunkist, aka Danica.

She held out her granola bar wrapper and said, "Miss Pat, where's the trash can?" All the leaders in my vicinity burst into laughter while she stood between me and the trash can, approximately two feet directly in front of her. At first, I thought she was kidding, but when I realized she really wanted me to locate and tell her where it was, instead of thinking for herself. I decided to play along answering her, "I don't know honey, I don't see one. Let's all look around here; there's gotta be one close by. Nope, I don't see one, I guess you'll have to hold it till we find one." All the leaders and I looked bug-eyed at each other when she actually got frustrated at me, stomped her foot and walked *away* from the trash can to go look for one.

We tried to squelch our laughter and began huddling with the program aides and all the leaders to establish a wording for the new ground rule about to be implemented. A few comments passed around the pseudo-conference circle of, "What the heck's really going on with these girls"? Then, we quickly formatted the mission statement and objectives to get these girls thinking on their toes. We were all on the same page and in agreement that we needed to hold the line on the incessant questions, other than safety issues, on a minute by minute, second by second basis.

The objectives we established were (1) to coach them into listening closely and carefully when instructions were/are being given and explained, (2) when they found themselves in doubt, they could look things up, research answers, ask a buddy, and try to think about if they might already know the answer to their question in the first place, and (3) to break the rote habitual dependency of expecting someone else to think for them all the time, which was the main objective.

Once agreeing on the objectives and guidelines, we gathered the troops into the dining space seating everyone at the picnic tables for a little pow-wow time. I agreed to tee it up with the basic announcements following the chore schedules, bunk assignments, and safety reminders. Our two Aides Pico and Thumbelina were naturally perched at my side. They would be our saving grace all weekend mentoring and monitoring while also being tasked to liaison between the generational gaps. They too felt the need to implement the new rule, also being overwhelmed with needless questions.

I began with the fundamentals by showing them where to locate master camp itinerary schedules posted on clipboards, and hanging on the inside walls of our dining space. They included chore rosters, bunk house assignments, safety rules and emergency plans, which would remain up all weekend for everyone's reference and benefit. During the opening orientation, there was a flood of "what else," questions! Launching like popcorn kernels in a pot of hot grease. The two PA's were looking at me smirking with anticipation of the feast to come. Thumbelina leaned in and muttered under her breath, "They are really going to love your next presentation," while I chuckled and softly answered back, "Aren't they, though!"

The leaders on the sidelines kept reiterating the same three word phrase trying to aid in the process, "shush, quiet down and listen." We passed out printed copies of the same information for personal reference, after covering the essentials of time schedules, reviewing emergency rules and exit plans.

It was now time to tackle the nitty-gritty issue of tabling questions! For their own good, we had to impart healthier listening skills and clarify the importance of paying attention or simply put, edify the importance and value of engaging their brains by exercising them whenever possible. This was a delicate process and subject, one that I knew had to be breached and discussed, but ever so softly like walking on eggshells around their blossoming delicate personalities. We didn't want to squelch their enthusiasm and zest for life, fun, and learning, we simply needed to redirect some unnecessary behaviors.

I began pretty much the same way I did in the car, "Girls, I need you to all listen up here for a few more minutes and really pay attention. I don't want to repeat information while you're talking to someone next to you, so please stop talking and pay close attention." They were getting squirmy and more than ready for launching into some fun activities of the camp, so leaders and chaperones had to jump in constantly refocusing their attention to polarize the side talk.

I soared right into the main objective by establishing the ground rule first, "Girls we are going to have a new rule this weekend at camp, which will be called the 'Think Before-You-Ask-AQuestion' rule." Moans, groans, and gasps filled the room affirming our suspicions; this was going to be a hard sell. This new concept of think first, ask questions later, wasn't going to sink in fast or easy for that matter.

"Stay with me for a minute girls, it's not as hard as it may sound, you might be way over thinking this, so let's look at it all together. This new rule simply means, before you ask one of your leaders and PA's a question, that you *might* already know, or have the answer to, or perhaps you may have a way of finding out the answers by looking it up, is that you try these things before blurting out a question.

Also, here are a few more things you could try instead of hollering out questions: you could ask a buddy if they remember or know the answer, you could think for a second, hmmm, 'do I already know this answer, and I just forgot it,' or you could simply look around and think about it for a few seconds and see if you can figure it out all on your own. In other words, try to figure out the answer to your question first, before trying to get someone else to do it for you."

This, of course, opened up Pandora's box with even more questions filling their gray matter with fight or flight responses. Most didn't even bother raising their hands; they were already down the rabbit hole, just shouting out their unrelenting questions, "but, what if we need to_____?" Fill in the blank; they were all the same, "but what if_____? What if?" This was a full-blown epidemic, and we were in triage trying to bandage all the bleeding questions.

Using my hands to catch the waves of energy pouring at us like a tsunami, I tried calming the storm again, "Okay everybody, hands down, quiet down and listen for a moment, please, this is what I'm talking about, right here! Guys, you don't need to panic here, you don't need to worry so much about thinking for yourselves, and you don't need to ask questions right now, really you don't, just breathe right now, and listen carefully for a few minutes. You'll get all the information you need, if you close your mouths, engage your brains and stay with me for a few more minutes. Now stop panicking, it's not necessary. Take some deep breaths, sit still, sit quietly and let it all in. I will take a few questions, one at a time, at the end, if I haven't given you enough information by then. I need everyone's attention, and patience, please."

They all stared back at me like I'd just taken away their favorite stuffed animal or something. I could see the looks of contempt on my own daughter's face like, "Why are you trying to rain on our parade today?" Pico and Thumbelina were holding up well, with their expressions of suppressed humor watching the drama unfold from the front of the room.

I continued slowly and with empathy, "I get it you guys; you are all overthinking this right now. Your brains won't let you hold onto all this information at once, and it's bubbling around and boiling over like a pot of hot oatmeal in your brains right now, I get it. I understand you want to get it out of there as quick as possible by having someone else take it from you and process it for you, I understand, you want us to think for you. However, we are all going to take a deep breath here, and we are all going to practice this together. This new way of listening carefully and thinking, and processing information for yourselves is all we're asking you to do this weekend, that's it, that's all we're doing here." Pausing to let each phase seep in slowly, before giving them too much to practice with at once.

Continuing to help them decipher the nuts and bolts of the methodology we were about to embark, I continued, "Now if all 45 of you ask a question every five minutes, all weekend long, that's 540 questions an hour, and that's too much for *our* brains to process! You guys have to help us out here and take some of the heavy thinking for yourselves. Everyone here is fully capable of doing so, and we are going to support you by doing this together. All the leaders and I are right here to assist you and facilitate if there's an emergency, but that's not what we're working on, so stop panicking through this process. We are going to help you by holding you accountable for thinking for yourselves, and by not answering stuff you already know the answers to, the stuff you have been given the information for already, or can figure out without our help, that's all that is going on here."

Then I paused to watch them process, and I noticed they still had the deer in the headlights expressions like, "What just hit us?" With the blank expressions, I knew we weren't out of the woods yet. This was a deep-seated problem, and we were busting it up like concrete. "Now everybody take a deep breath, settle down, listen, think, and stop letting yourselves get overwhelmed. This is *not* an emergency, so stop pushing the panic button. All we're asking you to do this weekend is think, besides have fun; we can do that at the same time!"

Although the mood was beginning to shift slightly, we still had quite a bit of work to do. They were on the edge of their seats now going into withdrawals, and I could feel the waves of energy proliferating to ask more question.

Gently I began again, "I will take a few questions if you raise your hands, and everyone stays quiet to listen for the answers. Perhaps someone else's question and answer will cover most or all of your questions at once." Then suggesting another new concept, I continued, "You might want to try taking out a pen or pencil from your backpack to write down questions that pop into your brain. If we don't answer your question by the end, then you can investigate to find the answers, and perhaps ask your friends and buddies if they can help you with the answers."

Opening the floor to questions triggered the proverbial avalanche of what if and emergency situations questions. The questions began firing again from the galleys, "so what if there is an emergency, then can we ask a question? What if someone is hurt or bleeding, then can we ask a question? What if we get lost on a hike can we ask for directions? What if we get sick can we ask to go see the nurse? What if we can't find our buddy? What if we see a wild animal, and it's about to attack us, can we ask a question then?"

I'll give it to them, they do have wild imaginations, and they do think about a mile a minute. If we can harness and funnel this thinking into solutions for themselves, well we will have something here. I jumped back in the saddle again, quieting everyone down and trying to calm all the fears at once, "Girls, let's cover what an emergency is, and when you *will* need to ask a question. An emergency is when someone gets hurt and is in pain, bleeding or not

breathing, if a fire breaks out, if someone is missing or lost, if someone is sick and needs to see the nurse, or if there is any danger
whatsoever that could be harmful to people, animals or the camp,
then you can and may ask a question. Does that help you answer all
your emergency questions?"

No, of course not, that was a silly question! They still came
up with a dozen more scenarios that all led back to the same basic
information I covered from the beginning. Yearning to squeeze out
a few more drops of juice from the elixir of bourgeoning questions
before laying to rest the subject of asking unnecessary questions.
Then we did it; we closed the floor to questions! It was traumatic, it
was dramatic, but it was closed! For the weekend!!

They were still breathing and staring back at me like looking at
a scary 3D movie. With everyone still quiet, I continued quickly,
"So, now that we're all set with the new rule and thinking policy,
can we go have some fun for the weekend?" They gave me a half-
hearted "yeah, yeah, yeah," to which I got them all on their feet,
"Come on girls, let's do this, let's rock this camp and have fun!!"
We dismissed them to go choose and set up bunks, with a quick
reminder for checking their schedules and showing up on time for
doing chores. They shuffled out of the dining structure like the wind
was completely out of their sails. I half-heartedly felt sorry for their
off-colored mood looking so lifeless, but I also knew the amount
of energy stores they possessed and how quickly they could/would
recover. I also knew I needed to preserve my own energy stores that
weren't quite as vast as theirs.

Pico and Thumbelina were musing to themselves, by the time
we finished, about how cute they looked wrestling with their own
untethered emotions and I praised them for keeping such a steady
profile while we worked through the process. The leaders and I took
a well-needed and much-deserved breather before another strategiz-
ing session, of which we raised our own new questions, like "do you
think this rule will actually hold up and/or actually work?"

We all most certainly agreed it would be a learning experience with growth spurts from both sides of the issue. We also agreed it would be challenging not to answer rote questions absent-mindedly, but it was important to keep a straight face when they pouted and reacted to our newly-formed union. Again, not because we were laughing at them, but because they were actually so cute wrestling with adolescence, and for the very first time in hours, we enjoyed the absolute peace, quiet and solace of not having to comprehend, decipher, or answer a question! Yes, it was an eerie quiet, like the quiet before the storm.

*

Then the fun began! The winds of change were in motion for sure, and it was like watching them learn to walk all over again. They filed into the dining hall with dozens of questions firing on autopilot, all of which they knew the answers to.

"Where is the cleaner for my cot? Do you want us to put our sleeping bags on the cots now or wait until bedtime? Are we going to make s'mores tonight? Are we going to practice our skits after dinner? Can I go to the bathroom without my buddy with me? Are we going to have a snack before dinner? What time are we going to eat? Can I move to my friend's bunk house that isn't in our troop? Can we take out the Frisbees and badminton stuff now? What are we having for dessert? Can we go on a hike after dinner? Why can't we ask questions? Do I have to eat salad if I don't like it? What if someone falls or gets hurt, or a wild animal is about to eat them, can we ask a question then?"

What are we raising here a bunch of trial lawyers, asked and answered already, like a hundred times, enough with the questions! However, we used our best poker faces, smiled and let them figure it out. Yes, they were in the thicket of growing pains learning to think for themselves, but so were we watching them do it. I couldn't help but wonder where all the questions and insecurities came from?

Did we condition this habit into them? Had we so blindly answered their questions so often without thinking first ourselves, if perhaps they already knew the answers? How was this whole scenario created? Were we letting them lean on us too long, while we did all the heavy thinking for them, slowing down and stunting their natural growth process? And did all groups go through this learning curve at this stage?

I wasn't sure where it came from, but I was certain of one thing, we needed to switch gears, and fast! These girls were on the cusp of puberty with some of them already there, and they needed to start thinking and making decisions for themselves in the real world soon. It was a bit concerning that they were in such short supply of confidence, not to mention turning our brains to mush. "This will be good, just give it a little time," I kept repeating the mantra to myself and others for support. For the most part, within a day, we were getting back to having fun, with the occasional trickle of questions still filing in, but nothing like the avalanche we experienced in the beginning. Now when the girls asked a question, a look would suffice instead of the earlier reminders of, "Is that a question?"

However, on the second day, I overheard the girls from my troop Tinker (aka Chelsea), Snoopy (aka Heather), Sunkist and Minnie Mouse talking about me, and the stupid rule! I truly felt sorry for their irritations, but I couldn't fix it for them, at least not in the way they wanted me too. This was a leap of faith, trusting they would figure it out with time. Going through the atonement was the first step, again for both sides, like watching the girls mocking me when they became frustrated and repeated my counter question around the camp in a condescending tone, "Is that a question?" In a tenor that said, "I can't stand this rule or the lady that introduced it."

I only wished I'd brought a video recorder to catch these darling behaviors. They were like miniature damsels in distress, over-dramatizing their grief about not being allowed to fire a question every ten seconds. Then it hit me; we *could* show them a video from our perspective. Perhaps using a method we played with my family on New Year's Eve that we affectionately called, doing impressions.

It evolved one year when my whimsical husband, who was as bald as Telly Savalas, walked into a family meeting doing an impression of our second oldest son Maxwell, who was sporting a popular beach-boyish hairstyle of flowing blond tresses draped over his face and covering one eye. Instead of pushing the hair back with his hand, or better yet with hair gel like I suggested, he would jerk his entire head in a circular motion, flicking his head backward somersaulting the golden locks out of view. I kept threatening to cut it off if he didn't find a more effective way of removing the hair from covering half of his face, to which he didn't seem fazed by at all, and completely ignored.

When my husband opened the meeting enacting the gesture by copying the move without a thread of hair on his head saying, "Who does this look like"? It brought down the house down. The kids were on the floor laughing in stitches, all except the kid who, of course, was the outsource of the fond impression. He was sitting with his arms folded smirking, "ha-ha, very funny."

Then my son sprang into action and said, "I have an impression too. Who does this remind you of?" He pretended to be lifting something and doing some manual labor, while taking deep breaths and then wiping his hand in one sweeping motion, from his eyebrows up to his forehead and circling over the top of his head, and back down the neck, then wiping his hand on the back of his pants. This was a move he'd seen dad do many times over the years, catching the sweat dripping into his eyes during times of exerting himself. After his academy award performance, he sat back down and responded, "At least I *have* hair to keep the sweat outta my eyes."

To which the room erupted in screams of laughter again! Being the good-natured person he was by starting all this banter, my husband responded through short breaths of laughter, "Touché Maxwell, touché! You got me!"

From there it evolved in our family, whenever someone had a behavior that possibly needed atonement, they would find themselves at center stage, as one of the stars of our ever-popular family fun night entertainment on New Year's Eve, doing impressions. Because from that day forward my son quit flicking his hair back with the jerking motion, and my husband tied a bandana around his head to catch the dripping sweat during manual labor. Through humor and laughter, we created a new way to show each other how we were experiencing one another, without using a diatribe they couldn't hear, directly speaking that is.

This occurred to me when I lamented over not having a video camera. Why not try something new we'd never done before at camp? Why don't the leaders submit a skit at the campfire gathering with all the other participants? We'd keep it light and humorous, while imitating some of the most exaggerated behaviors. Would it work? We didn't know, but we put together a list of some of the funniest incidences, like the trash can between Sunkist and me asking, "Do you see a trash can?" and then worked out from there.

It was time to circle up for campfire time with songs, skits, and s'mores. And, as the infamous Beatle Juice would say, "It's show time!" After the girls had performed their skits and songs, having a good time by all, the camp director announced there would be one more skit performed with a late submission by the leaders. The girls looked intrigued by this phenomenon, as I said, it had never been done before.

We titled our performance "She's A Happy Camper," and began introducing ourselves with fictitious silly camp names like, "Hi, I'm Taking Myself Too Seriously" and "Hi, I'm Not Sure, and these are our two friends, Why and Do I Have To, with our leaders, Gimme A Break, Are You Kidding Me and Really, and introducing herself is our camp director," (hands gesturing) turning it over to our final two cast members, Too Cool (which really was her camp name!) and Too Funny.

With character names somewhat describing our performance behaviors about to be displayed in full regalia, we brought down the house with the play on words in a full satire rendition of "Who's On First." The girls squealed with laughter as we played out the silly situations, especially seeing the adults acting so childlike with our fake whiny mannerisms, with the exception of the girls in my troop, who saw a bit too much of themselves in the recital. I tried not to look at them staying focused, but it was hard to miss them standing now at the back of the room, arms folded, feet tapping, stern-faced and the only ones in the room taking it all way too seriously.

Exiting the stage and walking back to our seats the room was still filled with applause. Reaching the back of the room near our seats, I glanced at the girls from my troop perched in a row standing just behind our chairs. Their narrow eyes and disapproving stares said, "Game on lady." Snoopy (my daughter) leaned in smirking, "We *don't* act like that," as they all marched to the other side of the room to glare at us for the rest of the program. Before they made their getaway, I smirked back, "Did you think we were imitating you guys, that wasn't you guys, really, 'cause you guys don't act like that, no way, that wasn't you guys."

After they had been out of earshot, I leaned over to Suzanne the leader seated next to me and said, "We must have nailed it, 'cause I think we struck a nerve." She tried to suppress the laughter, which only came out like a balloon bursting, contagiously affecting our entire row of actresses into uncontrollable chuckling.

Well, we did *not* have the last laugh with that narrative, and if imitation is the greatest form of flattery, then we had a standing ovation the next morning at breakfast! The girls were ready for us with their own rendition of "Who's On First" lassie style, with a satire twist of the seven dwarfs. After singing the blessing and just before chow down, Sunkist, Snoopy, and Minnie announced

SHE'S A HAPPY CAMPER

from the circle they had a little play skit to show us which would only take a few minutes. Looking at the other leaders like "What have we gotten ourselves into?" we all shrugged our shoulders and granted them the spotlight.

They called their production, "Snow What, I Have a Question," which started the laughter right out of the gate. We laughed so hard our sides hurt, seeing ourselves in full candor and sincerity, sprinkled with a tad of sarcasm and doused with over exaggerations. The openness with which they embellished our two-sided learning experience gave new meaning to the word touché!

They opened the sparring with introductions while cleverly harmonizing the names. "We'd like to introduce our troop leader, Snow What, and her sidekick Cantankerous and their seven scouts, and now we'd like you to meet, Shy, Dreamer, Confused, Jolly, Annoyed, Snappy, and Nurse."

Like lunging forward in a sword duel of swirling blades, they ended on a swashbuckling note wrapping the final scene with the skillful play on words. Confused and Annoyed running onto the stage, out of breath gasping, "Miss Snow What, come quickly, Jolly just fell down on a hike in the woods and she's bleeding, we can see the bone sticking out, she's crying, and we think she's broken her leg, can you come help us?" to which the leader replies, "Is that a question?"

Annoyed said, "I'm confused, isn't this an emergency?" And Snow What points to the other girl saying, "I thought she was Confused and you were Annoyed?" Then Confused huffs, puffs, and spouts, "I am Confused, and she's Annoyed," to which Snow What replies, "I'm confused 'cause I thought you were annoyed and..."

Jolly interrupts laying on the ground from a distance with her buddy Nurse at her side, shouting, "And I'm Jolly," with her buddy chiming in, "and I'm Nurse," to which Snow What replies, "She must be okay then," and Snow What walks away. They all stand-up, clasping hands in a row with the leaders first in line introducing themselves one by one bowing, "I'm Cantankerous," and they all bend forward, looking down the line, and shout, "We know you are."

The second leader, "I'm Snow What," they all lean forward looking down the line saying, "So what?" She answers back, "No, Snow What," and they answer back "So what?" And she replies, "Is *that* a question?" This brought roars of laughter, even from the leaders!

Then down the line, "I'm Shy, Dreamer, Jolly, Annoyed, Snappy, Nurse," and finally "I'm confused" to which they all lean forward and say, "Is that a question?" And Confused answers back, "Isn't *that* a question?" They all shouted and were done! Taking a bow together, to their peers and leaders, standing cheering, laughing and clapping the momentous closing of our no questions asked camp of learning how to think for ourselves!

We rode home in silence from that camp, feeling a sense of comfort and contentment in peacefulness and quiet time and knowing each other a bit better, and respecting the tutorials we received with humor, love, and laughter in the form of flattery and character building. The time flew by quickly on the return trip like it never had before!

CHAPTER 8
GET OVER YOUR BAD SELF

WHERE DID THE time go? Again, such a cliché, but so true. With what seemed like the blink of an eye, we were bridging up to Cadettes. The girls ranged in age now from about 11 to 13, and at this juncture, they had a multitude of extra-curricular activities. Their incredibly busy schedules included such things as hula, acting, hip-hop dance, choir, sports and church youth groups for most. With Girl Scouts not being anywhere near the top of the list for any of them, it certainly wasn't considered a cool thing to do among their peers at this age, and it was now rapidly becoming a closet activity, in which they didn't bring up or discuss around non-scouting friends.

After bridging up to Cadettes, nearly half the girls opted to quit altogether, while the other half decided to scale it way back with regards to meetings and earning badges. They were also becoming even more selective in choosing the few favorite events they wanted to attend. Such is the case of my own life with seasons, I too had defined my priorities, becoming more discerning with my time.

'Tis naturally the case for most people with age, and is a wise process. Nationally, the dropout rate is statistically much higher, and at a much younger age level, so looking back we were actually pretty lucky to keep them all together for as long as we did.

From this point on, the six that elected to stay had a very distinct plan for where they wanted to go, immersed with their own ideas, and assisting with steering the vessel. In the mix, there was of course my daughter Heather, miss bossy-knickers, cute as a button, tough as nails, fragile as a teacup, comedian, artist and performer, talented in acting, singing, dancing, golf, swimming, surfing, volleyball, equestrian riding, and snow skiing, while growing more and more resilient with her bubbling convictions about life.

Miss Kelcy, our talented and gifted resident artist, actress, singer, dancer, soccer, and tennis player, a nature lover, yet not so much an avid hiker, camper and outdoorsy type, however, flow with, flexible and adventurous enough to roll with the punches, while dabbling and trying new things! Soft around the edges and yet sturdy on the inside, adorable and durable done up in one package.

Miss Chelsea, our petite, shy, yet blossoming flower of sunshine! She could light up any room by merely walking into it, becoming quite the athlete with soccer, volleyball, basketball, baseball, swimming and surfing, while becoming the leader she was meant to be.

Miss Tanya, who is kindhearted, loving, hardworking and patient beyond her years. She was diligent to everything she set out to endeavor, dedicated and loyal to her basketball, family time, church and religious studies, with a salt of the earth character and calm, quiet demeanor.

Miss Danica, joining the troop during our Junior years as if she'd been there all along, is the persona of adaptability, quickly adjusting to every situation with everything and everyone she meets, with a well-rounded disposition, athletic and into a variety of sports much like her balanced nature, upbeat and fun all the time. She was one of our most helpful and unruffled young ladies.

Miss Erin, our newest and youngest member of the troop, was a bowl full of cherries and sunshine! She was the poster child of scouting with unwavering loyalty. Clear and secure to her beliefs, confident from within, and optimistic about everything. She was the breath of Aloha!

I often looked at them and saw the bubbly little toddlers we started out with, yet they were transforming into such capable young ladies, at times, right before my very eyes. Occasionally, they would take themselves way too seriously, however, not so much with me anymore. Thank goodness we had finally squared off and evolved away from that phase, with the added bonus of relaxing a bit more while in one another's company.

Somehow our relationships developed into me becoming more of a mentor and reminder figure than a leader figure. Of course, I was still the leader for all intents and purposes, but my roll had certainly and instinctively shifted as the girls took on more responsibilities. It is important to note here; I was continuously handing them the reins, where I watched from the sidelines, deciphering when to pick them up again for a little coaching and guidance. This was a delicate process while dealing with young women and their quirks (I smile), and a fine line to be constantly monitored, always respected and never crossed.

So, now I was a constant reminder figure of a few inherent facts of growing up and getting older, with the front runners being a priorities list and keenly developing focus skills when taking on more of life's responsibilities, challenges, and activities. They were juggling a lot more than I ever thought about at their age. The world was telling them to be, do, and try everything at once! Of course, we were doing this as well, starting with Brownies to develop and expand our minds with a wide range of interests and experiences. However, now I was telling them to land on something and to focus, decipher, and move with clarity, giving 100% to a couple of things, instead of 10% to a dozen things.

At this bridge, I was trying as much as possible to create and set up some organized fun! All work and no play makes us all cranky!!

Back to the, *let's not take ourselves too seriously* mantra, and balance it all out with work, rest, and fun! However, my idea of fun and theirs sometimes got lost in translation. Oh well, we still had the proverbial generation gap, while it was ever-so-slowly closing.

Of course, our saving grace for closing the gap with retention was having Crystal over the past couple of years. She was the cool role model preventing the last few girls from retreating altogether. I take no credit for keeping them involved during these years, other than to have the wise sense to bring Crystal aboard our leaky vessel. They loved, looked up to, and fondly wanted to be just like her when they grew up. Indeed, the last six did follow in her footsteps shortly after bridging up to Cadettes, with completing PA & PCCS training, which stands for program aide (PA) & Paumalu camping with a core staff (PCCS).

The second hook which piqued everyone's interest, and was helpful with retention, was electing to plan an adventure somewhere offisland as a troop trip. They could earn a travel badge learning about mapping out travel plans while budgeting and raising the money themselves. Later they augmented their plans by adding a service project in guardianship of the Girl Scouting traditions, and now the trek was back on track with regards to preserving and honoring scouting.

They were landing on their feet with a plan and taking on a new direction at the awkward tween stage in life with the need of supervision, though not so much of it up close and continuous anymore. We were rolling along smoothly down the river of life, with a breather to enjoy the view. However, we did have a few more rapids to cross. In other words, there was a ways to go before reaching the next bridge, or in terms of stepping onto the next rung of this ladder, we were all climbing it together.

*

A renewed confidence and enthusiasm followed with new directions, milestones, and goals. The first few meetings consisted mostly of brainstorming ideas for raising money, possible travel destinations, and feasible community service projects.

In fact, in the first year of Cadettes, the only things we did do and decided as a troop was, to stay all together (as a troop) for three more years, investigate and plan for a troop trip in three years with a service project, fill out all the pertinent financial paperwork with the Girl Scout Council necessary with fiduciary responsivities for holding over funds in our non-profit checking account for the next three years, and graduate PA & PCCS trainings at the council level.

These sessions and discussions carried over well into the second year while they saved and raised money for the aforementioned travels. Their activities focused more on staffing PCCS camps as a troop and attending troop meetings of younger scouts as PAs. In other words, being the angel with an extra set of wings, for another weary leader. Oh, to remember back in the days when I hung on by a thread until my PA (program angel) came along!

They all interviewed and chose younger troops to mentor, much like Crystal did with us in years prior. They undeniably earned and developed leadership skills while mentoring their younger twin sisters, who ironically whined and complained about their nerdy leaders. Yes, they had come full circle with this new adaptation of themselves. Looking back and remembering as Crystal did, only a few years earlier how wobbly they were at learning to balance their new emotions during adolescence. Yes, the time flew by quickly, and they were taking to the skies effortlessly ascending to new heights daily, soaring in their elements while I flew right next to them, catching the views from new vistas.

We all attended and staffed Paumalu camps together as a troop, with Pico and Thumbalina handing over the batons, training all the new recruits to replace themselves someday in the very near future.

This was the third and final hook keeping them involved during the not so cool years of scouting. However, at the camp, they were definitely in their domain! They were finally the cool older girls to be revered and looked up to. They were slowly moving forward, towards hero status with their younger contemporaries, as well as becoming the saving grace for leaders who so urgently needed their help, ideas, and energy.

It was the perfect layout for the older girls to practice, model and display grown-up behaviors in a responsible, safe and healthy environment with adult supervision. They evolved naturally into each level of the program, while maturing, growing and doing something worthwhile and fun with a purpose. As well as entertaining themselves and others, they gained invaluable experience with hands-on responsibilities, planning and running the activities with the adult staff. It was a win/win for all, all the way around.

Like their mentors before them, they were now the bridge between the younger girls, and their leaders as the hip, up and coming role models. They were at the prime age to take on a ton more responsibility and thrived on the autonomy. It was a marriage made in heaven, for all the girls and the younger troop leaders, who were now shifting gears into a much-needed role change as well. What more could anyone ask for? It seemed all my worries from the beginning were starting to fade away, or at the very least I wasn't holding my breath anymore.

I was also leading solo now, something I never thought I'd be comfortable doing. However, like the girls, I was evolving and increasing my horizons as well. Every year I was taking a few more baby steps while trusting and looking upwards more for my answers, rather than from within.

My husband was traveling a great deal of the time now for business, and missing out on most or all the events. Much like a single parent, I was taking on everything from our home, my career, the extra family activities, and my own newly added health issues. In other words, I wasn't sitting back on my laurels resting or just taking in the view. However, I could sit down a bit more often, and sometimes for longer intervals.

Yes, the girls were back on a roll again, having fun, growing with grace and ease, and I was enjoying myself watching the whole process sprout wings and grow. I felt so blessed to be on this ride with them. When we attended the camps together, my heart soared to see them in their prime. Seeing the independence growing on their faces as they took off hiking to the top campsites, which included all the perks and benefits, with the best views on the mountain top. The self-sufficiency they displayed through this liberation was priceless, purchased only with personal time, understanding and mentoring.

How many times had I questioned the process and if I was up for this task, worried if I was taking on more than I could handle or follow through with and constantly wondering what I was doing all of this for? And then I would see these girls soaring like eagles in their natural habitat, having the time of their lives, and all my doubts, fears, and questions disappeared into thin air, bringing up new questions like, what was all the worry about, and why all the fuss?

*

The startup of our second year as Cadettes began with a bit of drama, especially for my daughter Heather. Into the first month of meetings, my husband announced he was offered a job on the outer island of Maui, and he wanted to accept the position right away. He was adamant, knowing this employment step was a huge career opportunity. He also reasoned, it was only a thirty-minute flight from our home, and he could start right away while I stayed behind for a year preparing our family, the house and closing out personal obligations for the pending move.

In terms of the Girl Scout troop and the mix of life's decisions with all its twists and turns, we had the pending troop trip, in which to think about as well. A third of the money had already been earned and saved during the first year of Cadettes. With two years still left for completing our goal on the scout trip, along with all of our other personal obligations, this was rendering a heavy decision to make. Without much time to think, feeling pressured to give leeway with regards to my husband's work navigations, and the offer to quit my job for staying home full time to be a mom, I agreed rather hastily.

Our family plans were set in place with a sudden and urgent motion. The biggest wave of change would be dealing with Heather, who was about to enter high school as well as the clumsy stage of puberty. I also had my own health issues which were exposing themselves with time and age. I was still trying to dodge the bullet from the sixties, when we didn't even know what sunscreen was, much less use it. I was doing biopsies and chemo treatments on a regular basis for skin cancer, and only two years out after recovering from surgery with cervical cancer.

The house was 70 years old and had been manhandled by three teenaged boys growing up over the past couple of decades. It was in dire need of repairs and/or remodeling if we were to sell or even rent it out. These decisions were pending, while my head was still swirling from all the changes that would have to take place!

I would have to clean out and reduce the remnants of our five-bedroom home, of which my three older boys had moved out leaving all their belongings and treasures still housed and stored like a museum. I needed to research, set up and schedule construction remodeling work for the structural repairs right away and perhaps find a realtor for after the renovations. I also had to find a realtor for relocating to a new home on Maui and research and investigate movers for deploying our belongings and shipping automobiles.

Our community obligations ran just as far and wide as the house, and I would need to resign from the chair position of the school board at my daughter's school, and help transition my replacement. I would have to notify all my hair clients of twenty years and work individually with each of them while making and implementing the changes. I would also need to find new schools, churches, doctors, vets, horse stables, acting and dance classes, yoga studio, stores and marketplaces. I was about to climb Mt. Everest here, and we were on a slippery slope for sure. However, paramount and foremost I had to address my daughter's sensitive, emotional needs, and our Girl Scout troop goals immediately on the first things first list.

My husband accepted the position, packed up his office, shipped his car and flew out within four days of introducing and making a decision on this life changing event. I, however, was left standing in limbo with the aftermath of a teenager, in her world turning upside down. I didn't know how to address it with her, much less where to even begin. Numbness sank into every pore of my body from all of the changes and decisions happening so fast. To say I was overwhelmed, numb and confused was an understatement.

I sat down wanting to simply cry it out, giving up on all of it, but was afraid to let go of the first snivel for fear I would never get the dam to stop breaking, or get back on my feet. Keeping a stiff upper lip was the only way I could face the massive amounts of work piling up at my feet. I did sit down to breathe and meditate before it was time to make a more serious call, to the one upstairs!

"Dear Lord, please carry me through this next journey, because I don't know what to expect. Please give me the words that I will need, and the help along the way. Please open the doors smoothly for this transition of life, when you are ready to reveal to me what I am supposed to be doing here next and give me the strength, wisdom, and grace to help my daughter and family through those doors with me."

*

Trust was all I had left to move forward with, taking one step at a time towards the long road ahead. It felt much like having blinders on to navigate this path alone, which took a leap of faith daily. I had to tell myself each morning, first breathe, then meditate, and think only about what *has* to get done for today, and finally move carefully and slowly to get it all done. It was like I was moving in slow motion watching a movie of myself perform, as I prompted my way through it, with my thoughts.

It was time to face the girls, and the first thing on the agenda was to hold a meeting deciding the fate and future of our troop, with the girls' input. As these forces beyond my control would decide our destinies, I opened the meeting with, "Girls, we have good news, and bad news," to which Heather immediately erupted into tears. She already knew the bad news and had been sobbing uncontrollably for days.

She was understandably upset about the pending relocation of our home and family. However, all I could do at this point was continue. Holding back my own emotions that were also knotted up inside, as I began again, "The bad news is my husband has taken a job on Maui, and our family will be moving there at the end of this school year." Heather began picking up the pace with this information and was now full on bawling and hyperventilating, with all the focus turning towards her. The girls were extremely empathetic and doing their best to console her with back rubs, "awws" and "ohs," and showing her sympathy for her new plight.

I tried not focusing too much attention on her emotions during this juncture. We had several private conversations in this battle of wills, exhausting every argument with reason and logic, trying to help her understand the whys, but to no avail, it only made things worse, and we needed to keep her on the subject at hand. Yet I completely empathized with her pain and emotional suffering, while at a loss for words. I was completely immobilized and unable to reach her emotionally or spiritually, at this point in time.

I seemed to be in my own triage traveling back a million miles away to memories from over 30 years earlier during my childhood when my parents relocated me in the middle of my high school years. It was still throbbing at this moment, as though it was the painful day they put me in the car to drive three thousand miles away from my home. Away from friends, school, neighborhood, church youth group and everything I knew and loved up until this point in my childhood. At an age when I was only two years older than she was now. I could still feel these raw emotions imprinted on my soul, and coming up vicariously through her every wailing sound.

Precisely how and why I made the first stipulation agreement with my husband before we married and started a family together that we would *not* move our children around during their schooling years, also agreeing we would do whatever it took to keep them in one home, and in one place until they all graduated high school. He, of course, agreed at the time, and now reciting in the present that "things change, circumstances change, and people change. Isn't that what you're always singing in the Girl Scouts' theme song that says 'We Change the World' and 'Make New Friends'?"

"Yes, but *after* we give them roots in the nest," I lamented. "They don't need flying lessons while their still learning to balance," was my only defense. Like a trial attorney, he then tried throwing in a clever loophole saying, "We did say we would stay in Hawaii, and Maui is in Hawaii." To which I clearly knew this was not the agreement, nor a good offense. It was still a point of contention, and one I was also trying to work through silently with all the other upheavals.

I knew I had to yoga breathe and keep talking in order to push away these memories buried deep within my bones, or I would begin sobbing right along with her. I couldn't even glance her way, with what might have appeared to be totally unsympathetic and uncaring, was actually wrenching my intestines while reliving the painful past in these present moments.

Shifting gears to an upbeat note, I forged ahead with the topic of business, "The good news is I will be your troop leader for the rest of this year. The other good news is, if we decide to choose Maui possibly as our destination of a troop trip, I will already be living there, and we could considerably reduce the expenses of our trip, which would leave us more money to be used for excursions, a service project, and fun things. Let's think about it, let's investigate it, and talk more about it this year."

Heather was completely losing it at this point, wailing and shrieking uncontrollably. She couldn't seem to be consoled by the girls' reassuring comments like, "It's only a thirty-minute flight from here Heather" and, "Come on Heather, it'll be fun, it'll be an adventure!" These girls were wise and mature beyond their years with all the training and shared experiences. It was a comfort watching them support one another through life's growing pains, and it eased so many of my burdens as well.

They also offered to visit her in her new home, while everyone extended an open invitation anytime she wanted into their homes for a visit after the move. It was now time for moving the focus back to scouting and making plans for the troop trip, which simultaneously made it far easier to reel Heather back into balancing her feelings for the duration of the meeting. At least it got her off the subject of *My life's in imminent doom and danger, and the sky is falling*, which was absolutely true on both counts, even in an adult's world, much less a young adolescent's.

For the next several months, everyone in the troop contributed with research for the best airfares, ideas and pricing of things to do, service projects we might want to consider, and things of interest on the island of Maui, while I worked endlessly remodeling the house, closing down my business, implementing plans for our relocation, planning scout fundraisers, functions and holding the meetings.

After ample discussion, research and a vote, we almost unanimously ratified the decision to make Maui our troop trip destination. With Heather being the only dissenting vote, the troop moved forward, researching the outer island plans more seriously. I contacted the Rangers of Haleakala National Park Services about possibly doing a project at the summit of the extinct volcano crater. The park had a very delicate ecosystem with many endangered plants and animals at its 10,000-foot peaks. This was of particular interest to the girls, and we decided to research it further.

With the plans set in motion, we also researched and studied survival skills for overnight backpacking trips involving high elevations and low temperatures. We collected brochures, scoured websites, books and print materials from the rangers at the National Park Services. Lastly, we began calculating the costs involved, and the timetables necessary for preparing to take the trip the summer following our family's relocation, and at the end of our three-year journey as Cadettes. We also discussed a commencement bridging towards becoming Senior Scouts at this turn in the future.

The momentum was building all during the second year, and all the last minute details were firmed up, which included a cookie mom for the final year and push of the fundraising, and the other moms rotating and hosting monthly meetings for the following year in my absence. Heather would sell cookies from Maui helping the troop finish the final fundraising and her and I would travel back to Oahu, picking up her cookies when the time came for distribution.

We also planned to make some weekend trips back to our beloved island to staff a couple PCCS camps and attend some monthly planning meetings as well. On a side note, I also needed these visits for medical checkups as well, finding out there were only waiting lists for new patients with a Dermatologist or a Gynecologist. I couldn't even get into one of them with a referral, and this was weighing heavily on my mind with all the other details to sort out.

Finally, all the plans were falling into place, and by the end of the second year, we were set for securing the overnight backpacking adventure and service project. Once living on the island, I would investigate a few more details about some fun things to do around the island after they completed the Outdoor Survival & Backpacking badges and the Haleakala Service Project. Those plans could/ would be firmed up in the last year through weekend meeting visits, emails and meeting phone conference calls.

This trip would be our last hurrah together, our last cookie blaster party, and our last Bridging Graduation together. It would be the last time we had to make a decision of whether we were staying together for another three years of scouting, but I couldn't let myself go too far into the future now. I didn't want to think about the closing events, so I mostly tried to stay present, hanging onto each and every moment of these final few and precious days left.

We did some extra fundraising that year towards the trip, like yard sales, in which I was able to donate a great deal, considering the move, bake sales, the Aloha Run clean-ups at Aloha Stadium, and a couple of car washes. Heather and I stayed in our newly remodeled home all summer after school was dismissed, giving her another few months to let go.

We held parties and said goodbye to friends, brothers, sons, my grandson and Heather's nephew, Sadie, the horse who Heather share boarded, groomed and rode in shows for years. To our comfy home, and only place Heather could ever remember living, which cuddled all her thoughts, dreams, and memories.

These last few months skipped by quickly with the clock ticking, coupled with all the busy work of planning, still researching last minute details and the rush of an overseas inner-island move. By the end of that school year, I had put in more work, time and hours than it took to raise all three boys and a girl put together. And I was simply exhausted!!

*

The last month was here! Moreover, along with it came the final departing touches in our lives. All the details of the house commenced, with one more huge yard sale to get rid of the large pieces of indoor and outdoor furniture and completing the fumigation tenting required in the new rental agreement, new locks and keys made, contracts signed with new tenants, and a final clean out was done. Done, done, done, and checked off the list.

Eleven months of painstaking, grueling work of closing down my business and saying goodbye to all my co-workers and clients after two decades of creating, sharing and bonding in one another's lives, withdrawing and sharing in their grief, some of whom were now codependent with their hairdresser of twenty years.

I handed out diplomas for the last time, with one going to my own daughter, along with her graduating class at commencement services, followed by a celebration and festivities. A month later I turned over records to the new Chairperson and attended a special going away party to commemorate ten years of service on the Church and School Boards, and said goodbye to fellow members, good friends, and all our extended families.

I attended my final luncheon and played the final round of golf with my Tuesday morning foursome of twelve years. Reminiscing about our beginnings in the nine-holers group, we held one more therapy session about all the love, laughter and growth we shared during our assemblies at the 19th hole, after a little fun, sun, exercise, adjustments, and atonements on the course, of course!

I shut down my parenting classes and attended one last party with everyone associated with its production in attendance were some past alumni, police officers, fellow teachers from across the island, and my partner Art from the Hawaii National Guard, who

127

was trained and had assisted me in teaching the copyrighted curriculum for five years.

I went to my last yoga class and said goodbye to all my fellow yogis and teachers who stood beside me every step of the way to finding peace, solace, and healing in so many areas of life with health. This was and remains today the hugest blessing and part of my healing process, both mentally as well as physically. Since they are so interconnected, that would make perfect sense!

We had closing parties to attend and sealing emotional goodbyes with work, play, family, and friends, right up to the last day, squeezing every minute out of each agonizing departure, ultimately closing a chapter of our lives on our way to Maui where a new door was opening. I (we) had to trust my husband's decision making by letting him follow his career path and stepping with him through this door.

Heather had school starting on a Monday morning following our last day on Oahu. I put her on a flight the night before so her dad could get her to school the next morning. I would take the afternoon flight with the cats, and be there in time to pick her up from school. The dogs were already there, taking an earlier jaunt with dad, being kenneled in a home, until I arrived to care for them. All I had left to do was wrap up the last-minute details in the house with the realtor, one last stop to do the final checklist, and turn over the keys before I was on my way to a new life!

Walking through the rooms in the final inspection, I finally realized and recognized it was all absolutely perfect, every inch of it, for the first time since we owned it. Like a shiny new penny beaming with pride. The echoes off the walls from the tile floors and empty rooms were billowing in my brainwaves. I couldn't seem to focus on the checklist without contemplating a trip down memory lane. We finally finished the examination so I could retreat to my car before I burst into tears.

I sat motionless in the driveway, looking at it for the last time, remembering how my heart and soul went into every inch of every corner over two decades of my life. I sat there wishing that we could have had it all that perfect when the kids were growing up there, or at the very least, that we could share it with them now. Then, like a wave of emotion, I could feel a heartbeat coming from the house as if it was saying, "Thank you for putting me back together." I had an inkling it was my own heartbeat throbbing, but it felt like waves of energy surging our life forces together as if we were connected by an umbilical cord transmitting messages and abducting my thoughts.

I could hear the voice getting louder with momentum, and clearly, it was shouting, "Hey there. Stop. Come back here. We are not done yet!"

Yes, the house was speaking to me saying, "Thank you for restoring me to my original state of beauty. Thank you for the new doors, windows, screens, floors and fixtures. Thank you for letting me hold your family through all its growth, pain, love, laughter, excitement, tears, parties, adventures, milestones and stories galore. And thank you for letting me be a part of your lives, sharing in your dreams, and supporting you with all your changes."

The house was truly coming up with these clairvoyant thoughts, because I was just sitting there leaning on the steering wheel bawling with nothing left to give, nothing more to dream, and it went on to say, "I held you up and supported you the best that I could. I sheltered you when you needed me to. I stored all your treasures that were near and dear to your hearts. I celebrated with you and your family's accomplishments, in the milestones as well as your losses and changes. I did my very best to heal those sadnesses of the past, and tried to replace the deficits you felt never staying in one home while growing up."

Even though I had a plane to catch, I just sat torpid, like telepathically I could feel the house breathing for me. It was taking on an energy, with a life force of its own, and now like an angel mending my broken wings, I felt the house was lifting me up in spirit saying, "It's okay now, it's okay to be sad, you can let go, and I will hold your memories here forever. They are safe with me now, encased within my walls, underneath my roof and part of this permanent structure. All the pets that you have loved are still here in spirit, along with their remains laid gracefully within my grounds. All the birthday parties, graduation celebrations, Christmas mornings, Halloween parties, Easter egg hunts, Thanksgiving dinners, sleepovers, scout meetings, sports events, first dates and proms, baby and wedding showers, funerals and memorial services, family meetings, games, growth, love, laughter, dreams and creations are still within these walls and will be sacred with me forever, with your karma, your spirits, your love and life's lessons."

I had to get out and walk through this time zone one more time, feeling I might never have another chance to look closely at the details and see the memories with all the scars that we left behind. Walking up the driveway, I traced my hands over the footprints etched into the concrete. Running a finger over the M.A.S.H. acronym scribbled below it, representing the names of my children, and the four lives that grew here, Maxwell, Andy, Stacy, and Heather.

I outlined the graffiti carvings on the tree house walls and admired the handiwork my eldest son Andy had put into it, remembering how proud he was, that he built all three levels without a single nail into the tree. I could visualize the boys hanging off the top deck wearing their pirate gear at the two middle boys' birthday parties and recall the morning I found Heather and her friend Amy sleeping inside it when they weren't in her bed and all the screaming, shouting and laughter that echoed from this spot.

I picked a rose from the garden Heather and I planted when she was just a toddler and walked back into the house, this time really taking in the fragrance that lies beneath these walls. I soaked up the beauty of the wall mural Andy painted behind the bar with banana trees, red ginger, and birds of paradise, and I beamed with pride looking at the artwork, appreciating its gifts. Doing the same with the horse mural Heather painted on her bedroom wall while reminiscing about the walls lined with all her riding ribbons that circled the entire ceiling. I traveled to Maxwell's abstract black and white décor wall and laughed to myself while picturing the drum set sitting in the corner, and all the hoopla with my musicians over the years. Those musical vibrations are surely encased here forever!

I admired the bookshelves Andy built in my office to hold all the photo albums that documented our lives, again noticing his artistry, handiwork, and gifts. Moving into the living room and feeling the smooth stones of the fireplace hearth I had laid and grouted myself, I had a chuckle about the memories of reading spooky Hawaiian stories by the firelight with the kids, and all the discussions that followed.

Before leaving, I felt the lines scratched onto the wood in the hallway with everyone's heights and ages, from milestone birthdays, including the parents that everyone aspired to pass up! These walls certainly held memories. This home was my life and my family's life for almost two decades, all stored up in one sanctuary. And this shelter seemed to be saying, "Thank you for pulling me through this triage and putting me back together. And thank you for honoring my gifts to you," in such a thunderous voice that I could not explain it, and I could surely not ignore it. So, I answered the call right out loud, giving voice to the call, "You are welcome, and goodbye my friend!"

I felt so lost during the plane ride and couldn't help but look back at my life, and how this moment was such a turning point, thinking about how I had carefully planned out my life, with all my dreams, and how I'd hoped it would go. I had dreamed of how I was going to keep my children in the same home growing up, something I had never experienced, and how I would give them roots that I never had. I had thought about how they would grow up, move out and start families of their own, to return with their children, and we'd reminisce on visits. I had dreamed of watching my grandchildren playing in the treehouse where their parents once played, how we'd all take them out on the kayaks for ocean adventures like we did when my kids were young, and we'd put them to bed in their old rooms. I envisioned a time when I wouldn't be rushing to work, but playing with them and their kids. I had so many plans and dreams for my life, and then along came God's plan for my life. So, let's just say we go with God's plan because mine just seemed to go poof.

It felt like my heart was breaking and shattering into tiny pieces and there was nothing I could do to stop it, so letting go and feeling the absolute pain of it all was the only thing I could think to do, then trying to move into trust. I had to trust that this was my path and the one I was supposed to be on because this is where I was, trying to trust as much as our two precious kitties that were sedated in the cargo hold. They were absolutely trusting me right now, and I was anxiously trying to find mine. And, after I located it, I needed to turn trust into faith, that this was where we belonged!

It was perplexing, leaving my island home of twenty years, and it was much more difficult than I ever imagined it would be. The feelings and sensations were overwhelming at this scary place of 20,000 feet without my dreams. All that was left now was discovering the faith that I needed, for pushing forward and letting this aircraft be my wings for now!

CHAPTER 9
TAKE A HIKE

T AKING A BREATHER while getting settled into my new home, I vowed no more whys or why me's. There was just moving forward, one step at a time, trusting that everything would be alright, and just as it was supposed to be. Still, it was a leap of faith, and easier said than done while sometimes a work in progress!

After a short settling in period, I got to work right away, so as to quickly heal amid what seemed like an open, gaping wound from all the emotional disconnect and also to act in concert with my new personal vow. First, this meant contacting the park rangers at Haleakala National Parks Service to discuss setting up, and doing our service project the following year. They had a plethora of ideas and were eager to be working with our scout troop in the very near future.

I also explained about some of the badges the girls wanted to earn in backpacking, eco-environment, and outdoor survival. They put me in touch with an organized volunteer group who conducted monthly service projects in the park, as a place to start. They suggested that I get my feet wet by going out with the volunteers to begin laying the groundwork for setting up the service project.

I wanted to learn as much as I could about the summit, the history, the elements, and the treasures that lay atop her mysterious mountain peaks. However, mostly I wanted to be sure of what I was getting myself into. I needed to know what to expect every minute from this mountain if I was going to take these young girls on an overnight backpacking adventure in almost freezing temperatures. But most of all, I needed to know if I could hike 16 miles in two days, carrying a 30 to 35-pound backpack. It actually scared me more than I was even willing to admit to myself, much less say out loud.

Yes, I knew of the actual dangers involved, having an idea of how difficult it could and would be. However, when I said I could relate to Kelcy on the whole outdoor survival badge thing, I wasn't just kidding, and now I was the one cringing over stretching my wings, having only one small overnight backpacking experience under my belt, and nothing at such a high elevations to compare it with. I called the number from the parks services and volunteered right away.

I spoke with a wonderful gentleman named Farley who said, "Oh yes, we do service projects every month at the summit. As a matter of fact, we have one coming up soon. We'll be hiking in ten miles the first day, and staying overnight at a cabin, hiking out the next day about three miles to extract some invasive weeds which are threatening the endangered silversword plants, among others, checking some Nene nests, feral traps, and hiking back to the cabin for the second overnight, then hiking nine miles to the next cabin and resting overnight. In the morning, we'll be cleaning and painting the second cabin, and hiking out approximately four miles, up a 4,000-foot cliff called switchbacks, to climb out of the crater and go home".

I gulped under my breath saying, "What the heck have I gotten myself into this time?" Then shocking myself even more by saying, "Please send me the info to sign up for this crazy tour!" What was I thinking? I don't want to hike thirty miles in three days carrying 30-40 pounds of gear. Am I losing my mind or what? I'm nearly 50 years old, this is just crazy talk, that's what this is! And the self-talk digressed from there!

Farley took a breath and said, "Have you ever done any backpacking before? Have you ever been to the summit of Haleakala? And does this sound like something you would like to do?" I answered all three rapidly, "A little overnight backpacking, one to be exact; yes, I visited the summit a long time ago, sixteen years ago to be exact; and yes, I'd like to do this, with my husband and daughter joining me," to which he asked, "How far was a little backpacking, how long was your visit at the summit, and how old is your daughter?" I felt like we were playing ping pong with the Q&A's in threesomes, "Backpacking was only once on an overnighter, for about three miles, carrying about 20 pounds, my visit to the summit was just at the lookout for about thirty minutes, and my daughter is 14," I responded.

Clearing his throat abruptly, Farley answered very sternly, "I don't take children that young up to the summit, I'm sorry, this is no place for a teenager that young, and I've tried it in the past, it has never worked out well. Once they get tired, cranky and can't handle it, their whining and complaining wears everybody down, and then we get nothing done. I'm *not* ever taking that on with a work project again. I'm sorry, I can't have your daughter go along. If you and your husband still want to join us, you are welcome, and that's all I can offer you right now."

Looking for a miracle now, but reaching for diplomacy, I began, "I do understand what you're saying, and I completely agree, this is a very serious endeavor, and I wouldn't suggest you take her on your project without knowing what you're getting into." Going into the brief story about the troop trip, badges and goals, I explained all the reasons why we wanted to try this project with an experienced group first. Farley listened quietly and still objected regarding Heather's age.

Making a final appeal, I went on to suggest perhaps he could meet with her before making a blind decision. Or perhaps, reassuring him that my husband and I both would be on the hike, and we would take full responsibility, leaving early without any disturbance, if she became unruly, despondent or difficult in any way. Again, he listened quietly and shifted slightly on his thinking.

"Okay, here's the deal. I'll let you bring her along since she does have a lot of camping and hiking experience with the girl troop. You and your husband are completely in charge of her at all times, getting her out of there, if there's the slightest problem, upon my request and you'll have to sign a waiver and agree to it in writing ahead of time."

"Yes, yes, and yes!" We were back to ping pong answers, and I was taking Heather along backpacking! "Thank you so much. I promise this will work out just fine, she is a delightful young lady, and mature beyond her years!" Well, the delightful part was true anyway!

I did sign up for the crazy tour to learn about the wiles of the national park, after recruiting my husband and daughter to go along, making it a family adventure. They agreed nearly as quickly as I did in the beginning, knowing we needed to practice up for the troop trip in the coming year while never divulging any of my own fears of taking on such an immense task.

Weeks later, upon careful and thorough examination of the full scope of work involved in this project, Heather and her dad started to get cold feet the closer we got to the departure date, especially after we filled our backpacks with 20 pounds of gear for practice hiking drills once a week, walking several miles, and increasing the weight and distance, to be ready for the feat.

Three days before the hike Heather started whining and complaining when she picked up her backpack, citing it was way too heavy to walk down the street, much less carry 30 miles on a mountain. When I tried using a little reason and logic to re-enlist her initial excitement about attaining her dreams and goals of earning the survival badge, eco badge, and backpacking badge, she only got worse, running down the hallway to her bedroom yelling, "This is child abuse, there are labor laws against making children walk that far, and doing manual labor. I'm not going to carry that backpack thirty miles, and you can't make me, that's all there is to it," slamming her bedroom door!

Once Heather started resending her enthusiasm for the trip, my husband went full on mutiny, hands up, "That's it, I'm out. Count me out. I'm done!" And Houston, we have a problem!

It was two days to go until the volunteer project. I had purchased and packed all the gear in all three backpacks, confirmed with Farley we were onboard with the other five volunteers, and both of them joined forces digging in their heels, with a full-blown retreat.

I opened up the dialog with my husband first, "So what do you want me to do now, call up Farley and tell him you guys are getting scared, and we can't go?"

"Tell him anything you want to, I'm not going if she's not into it, and that's, that. This is not for me; this is her deal, not mine." I took a deep breath here and paused, because we were on a very slippery slope now, without ever having set foot on the mountain.

"Yes, this *is* her deal, and that's the reason we do it! This is her dream, and her goal, but if we sit idly by and watch her fears take over right now, she'll never move past them, she'll never amount to anything more than her fears, and she'll stop herself, giving up on her dreams, every time a little fear steps in. Come on, how many times in your life have you let fear run you? I have fears about this too, I'm just *not* letting it run me anymore, that's all. We have to support her, we have to encourage her, we have to push her up to the plate sometimes, and we have to do this now, or she'll never push past her fears or amount to any more than her fears. Is that what you want for her? I say we lead the charge up that mountain and support her goal and dreams of getting those badges because it's not enough to just *want* them all your life, and wish you'd gone and tried to get them. She needs to *earn* these dreams, and we can't give up on her any more than letting her give up on piano lessons because she was afraid of a recital or giving up riding lessons when she fell off a horse. This is no different; we need to be next to her, and show her how to face her fears, not run from them."

He looked at me long and hard for several minutes, and then finally grinned, "Dammit, I wanted to ride in on her horse with this one, I'm getting too old for this stuff," to which we both laughed, and agreed to being a bit fearful, besides being passed our primes. Then, reinforcing my case, "All the more reason I have to do it first. Before I can take six of them into a mountain wilderness, I have to know I can do it first!"

He got on his horse and rode in to save the day, encouraging Heather to do the hike with us, and earn the badges with our help and support. She reluctantly agreed to go, if we agreed to nearly the same terms Farley laid out with getting her out of the summit if she didn't like it, or got too tired. We all agreed to her terms and set out together on the journey of a lifetime!

I have to admit here, I was a bit worried about Heather at the beginning of this hike. However, all my instincts pointed towards the training I knew I'd put into her and our troop of nine years. From here on out, I would have to trust that we had done all of our homework!

The minute Heather and Farley met, her training revived into high gear. Right away she was polite, articulate, and interested in all he had to say about the delicate ecosystem, animals, history, and rules of the park. She asked lots of questions, to which I was a bit worried at first that it might get on Farley's nerves. When I apologized if she was asking too many questions, he responded with an enthusiastic, "I love it. I'm so glad she is interested, and she listens very well. I can tell she is really interested in learning about the mountain, the plants, and animals, very refreshing for her age, we'll see how well she does when we start hiking and working?" We left it up to results and started making our way to the trailhead at 10,000 feet.

With a photo start, we were off; eight volunteer strangers and two volunteer guides on a three-day hike into a volcano crater, in which less than 1% of the world's population will ever experience in a lifetime. I felt excited, scared, blessed, apprehensive, strong, curious, exhilarated, and worried all in the span of about fifteen minutes, or the first half mile. I figured I'd be exhausted in the next nine and a half if this array of emotions kept firing and flaring up.

My thoughts finally settled down and fears completely vanquished when Farley and Heather began communicating like they were old college mates, leading the charge to the first cabin. He was delighted teaching her every minute detail of every inch of the crater. Ten miles passed quickly for them, getting acquainted on this stroll through the park.

I, on the other hand, was struggling just a bit, wearing a novice pair of boots that didn't quite fit properly. I also discovered much too late, that hiking long distances and long toenails don't a match make. Luckily, I borrowed a pair of clippers when we reached our shelter for the night, however, much too late to stop the intense pain that had already taken its grip. The throbbing nail pain increased and lasted the entire trip, and I was now forewarned by Farley that I would be losing those toenails within a week or so of our excursion (for which I couldn't wait). I did later lose three nails to be exact, and the pain I survived was a close second, only to giving birth to four children. Lesson learned and duly noted, I pushed through the hike vowing never to make this mistake again.

The second morning we hiked out about two miles for the first project of pulling invasive weeds near endangered plants. Since it was Easter weekend, I couldn't resist bringing along some camouflaged colored plastic eggs I found in the store while shopping for hiking essentials. On the hike to the worksite, I gave Farley the heads-up about having them in my backpack, and my plans to hide them for Heather before getting started on the project. I also let him know I had put ones and five-dollar bills in them, and he was also amused by the scheme.

Once we arrived at the location, he helped with distracting her while I placed them in a section he would later assign her to work on. I laid them openly on the flat ground since they were so cleverly cloaked blending into the terrain. Once she got to her task of weeding, it took about five minutes to finally notice and pick up one, by which time everyone in our work party was privy to the joke.

She didn't know what to make of it, and walked it over to Farley, checking to see if he knew what it was? He picked it up, rolling it around in his fingers and said, "It looks like an Easter egg to me," while handing it back to her saying, "Why don't you open it, and see if there's anything inside it?" She popped it open, becoming 5 years old again, when she exclaimed, "There's money in here, oh my gosh!"

Running over to her dad and me for show and tell, giggling with excitement, "Look, Mom, Dad, what I found on the ground over there!" We smiled, giving her a quick pat on the back, not giving away the full Monty just yet, and responded, "Wow, how cool is that?"

She went back to work rather quickly, thinking the excitement was over and the prize was in the bag. It took her another 30 seconds to spy a second egg, this time promptly opening it to discover the treasure inside! Shouting this time to everyone in the group, "Look! I found another one! Oh my gosh, this one has five dollars in it, oh my gosh!" waving the currency like a flag.

Taking a few more steps she found the next one, and now she was on a roll, "Look, Mom, Dad, I have four of them," holding them out like she just found the goose that laid the golden eggs. Everyone on our expedition was now enrolled into this playful tradition of an old-fashioned Easter egg hunt atop Haleakala mountain, camo-style.

She gathered eggs for another few minutes exclaiming the prize each time, with as much enthusiasm as the first. She enrolled our group with becoming young at heart, by simply watching her dash around with laughter and amusement. Finally correlating how the eggs must have arrived on the desert floor, she came over to give me a hug and thank me for the fun of finding them.

She also wanted to know if she found all of them so she could stop hunting. We counted them to discover one was still missing. Everyone joined in the search making it a complete dozen for her collection while rendering us all back to the service project, with a smile on everyone's face. There's nothing like a little fun and game time, to start up a serious weed pulling project.

By the end of our three-day extravaganza, we were exchanging contact info, and making friends for life. Farley paid Heather one of the greatest compliments I've ever received about her, saying "Your daughter has restored my trust in working with teens again. She is wise and mature beyond her years, and you have done a great job with her. You are welcome anytime you ever want to come to the summit with us again, and please bring her back, in fact, if you ever make it over to Hana, please look me up, I'd be happy to show you around there as well. It has been my great pleasure to meet and work with your family, and I thank you especially for bringing Heather along. She added a great deal, making a success of our work and trip, with her input and work contributions."

I was stunned and pleased, all in the same breath with this report, however, I couldn't have been prouder at that moment, than if she had earned a gold medal at the Olympics. She surprised and surpassed any expectations and wishes I had for her, to gain something fruitful through this challenging maze. On the drive home, we all talked and shared about the three-day event, the things we learned, the fun things we did, and great people we met.

Just before reaching the driveway to our home, I asked Heather to take her shower first, eat while Dad and I also cleaned up, and we would have a quick meeting together before bedtime. I gave her three questions to think about and contemplate for our meeting time. We would all then discuss and share our answers after unpacking and getting settled in. The questions to reflect on were:

(1) What was something new you learned about yourself this weekend? (2) What three things did you learn about the mountain and the ecosystem that you didn't know before? (3) What was your favorite thing about the mountain?

She was so excited sitting on the couch, bursting to give us answers before we could even get into the room. Never before have I seen her so excited to talk to us! Parents, maw, the people who embarrass her by giving her a hug in public. She wanted to talk to us, and with enthusiasm! This was such a switch in roles, with her now hurrying us to come sit down in the room to talk! It seemed we had now discovered her creative buttons, her motivators, and her passions in a place we had to coax her to go looking for it. That was a twist even I completely didn't see coming!

"So let me tell you what my answers are," she began before I sat down on the couch. "I learned that I can do way more than I think I can, like walking thirty miles. It didn't seem like all that big of a deal when I was doing it a little each day, and talking to people, and having fun and everything. Now I know I can walk that far, and even further if I wanted to keep going." We further augmented the discussion by talking about the initial fears that came up and how she walked them out, by doing and staying with her first goal, and not letting the fear run her or stop her from achieving her dreams.

The next answer was bubbling over with omg's, as she

continued, "and I learned so many things about the mountain I can't stop at three. I learned that Haleakala has the most endangered species of all the national parks. I learned the ecosystem has alpine shrub lands, desert lands, and cloud forests all within a few miles of each other and the 80 degrees in the flats really feel like a desert, and the 40 degrees at night is really freezing. I learned about the uau birds, and how they nest on the ground, mate with only one bird for life, and have only one chick at a time, and how they only live in Haleakala, Moana Kea and some summits on Kauai and Lanai, and nowhere else in the world and how they sound like flutes when they sing at night. Oh my gosh Mom, I learned so much, I can't wait to tell my science teachers tomorrow about all the things we did and saw, it was so cool!"

Number three was also spilling over, without being able to choose only one, "I don't know what my favorite thing is, because all of it was my favorite, like hiking up the cliffs, and looking out over hundreds of miles, over the ocean, finding the goat head with the full horns; hanging out in the cabins by candlelight and playing cards, and talking with everybody, and oh my gosh, finding the camouflage Easter eggs with the money in them. That was so cool."

We reminisced about our hike all the way up until bedtime, recalling the amazing sunsets, stargazing, views, sounds, and the lack thereof, with the most glorious sunrises we'd ever seen in our lives. We hit it out of the park on this hike and had an experience we'd never forget.

Taking her to school the next morning was as new as the mountain dew we trampled on the morning before at the summit. Every morning since we had arrived on this island, our new home on Maui, I had admired the majestic peaks of the mountain views on our drive to her school. I could never get her to look up and notice with me, or even engage in a pleasant conversation about the wonder and beauty of this magnificent monument. In fact, all I ever got was insolence and indifference, with a quick, "yeah, yeah,

yeah, Mom, I see it. It's a mountain, I've seen it before," staring at her newly acquired cell phone, playing with its fascinating new feature of texting!

After several months of these prompts and dialogs, I stopped talking about the views altogether, when she finally asked me to refrain by spouting, "I know it's there mom! I can look when I'm ready if I want to." We usually drove in silence, except for the constant beeping noise coming from the obnoxious touch tones of the phone.

This morning was different; this morning was amazing! We could see the white oracle sphere of the observatory like it was sitting in our backyards. She laid her phone down, turning towards the mountain, and exclaimed, "Look, I can see the science center ball. It's so clear today, wow. It's hard to believe we walked thirty miles up there this weekend."

My heart leapt at this moment, knowing how much her world had just expanded, knowing she now had a connection with this mountain, with nature, and was taking a very important step towards becoming an adult. I also knew she could now make the connection that her dreams matter, her goals are important, and her fears are just temporarily masking her real potential in life. I knew we were on the way towards getting her over the next massive step of adolescence, and into young adulthood.

We drove that morning in conversation, instead of the annoying sounds emanating from the bleeping phone. We shared and talked about our experiences some more, like it was all her idea, all along. Well, truly it was, inspired by her at least, because I would never have made this leap on my own of trekking thirty miles into the wilderness, discovering such a majestic place, if not for the wonderment and dreams of her imagination first. Yes, I truly felt blessed to be on this ride with her now, in this place, taking on new challenges, new horizons, and having new conversations with my own, ever so talented and excited daughter!

*

It was time for the step of setting up and finalizing plans for the troop trip. We began with purchasing airline tickets first and securing the travel dates to align all of the activities following our service project. Next came setting up the project and dates with the National Park Service and working with one of the rangers to coordinate our timing. Finally, on the to-do list, it was time for deciding, booking, and paying for the fun touristy stuff we always saved for the end to celebrate and reward ourselves in a traditional fashion of ending the year with a blast!

Number one on the touristy list was a boat excursion out to the extinct atoll of Molokini for some fun in the sun, snorkeling and barbequing, ocean style. This would be booked for some much-needed water and relaxation time, the first day after our summit hike and service project. Next on the hit parade of amazement, we booked the eco-hike and zip-line adventure on Haleakala Mountain, followed by an upcountry tour on the third day, to the historic paniolo (or cowboy) town of Makawao, a visit and tour of the Lavender Farm, Tedeschi Vineyards, and lunch at Ulapalakua Ranch's General Store and Grill. Wrapping the week up, we planned a day at Big Beach in Makena, and a shopping afternoon at Queen Kaahumanu Mall. Finally, if time and money permitted, a spa day including massages, manicures, and pedicures.

This was going to be a full itinerary, a week to remember, and a whirlwind tour for sure! However, the girls still had a lot on their plates before the travel, packing, and fun would commence. They still had all the prep work to do, learning the ropes of planning ahead, and getting it done on a time schedule. In English, this meant cracking open their badge books and completing some vital homework for earning the badges, executing paperwork for the Girl Scout Council and submitting signed documents before the deadlines. The latter being of huge importance to be eligible for traveling on an official troop trip, with troop funds.

They were also supposed to be in training, putting on the weighted backpacks and practicing walking several miles a week. Also, on the task list was collecting and checking off the items needed from the essential supplies list and lastly writing out the information they learned in their research about why they needed such items on a high-altitude hike, with maximum and sub-freezing temperatures, where there is no water supply. In other words, it wasn't enough to be told this stuff, and not enough to tell me they know this stuff, but they also had to write it down and show me on their paperwork.

This was not just a walk in the park, have some fun, and fly home kind of deal. It was about learning while having fun for sure. However, first and foremost, it was about being safe, following rules, paying close attention to details, and staying alive kind of deal also. Like getting all our i's dotted, and all the t's crossed in the planning stages with preparations first. Yes, fun was on the list, mixed in with exploration, research, survival, communication, and a commitment to excellence for leaving this habitat better than we found it on our journeys.

At this point I got to be the nag, instead of the guide, to make certain all the homework got executed and done. Therefore, I was not wildly popular. Nevertheless, we had to be diligent before we could do the fun stuff, and these are the woes of growing up, and not having the leader do everything for you! Heather and I traveled back to Oahu during the middle of the year to staff a PCCS camp, hold a meeting, check in with all the homework, and assist with the final push.

We had one more meeting together, with a trip planned to Oahu for Heather and me, in which we would complete the final paperwork together and do a last-minute details checklist/planning session a week before they could finally get on the plane and travel to Maui. During the week leading up to this last planning meeting, the girls began emailing one another with their doubts about doing the sixteen-mile hike and overnighter.

Heather apprised me of the communications, and the skepticisms being discussed via the internet. She started the dialog with me, by declaring she didn't want to do the hike or the project with the way the girls were talking. We were a week out from travel time for the last meeting, and I needed to know exactly what was going on with the girls and their thinking.

So, I gently sat down for a little Q&A time with Heather, and inquired with a light, whimsical air in to the questions, hoping not to offset her, or back her up into a corner. "Soooo, what do they want to do, if the consensus is they don't want to do a service project and hike at the summit?"

She was all too helpful, jumping right into the heart of the matter, letting me know exactly how we needed to change up this program right now, "Well," she began matter-of-factly, "they just want to skip the hike and the service project, still do the rest of the stuff and use the rest of the money for shopping and a spa day."

I simply smiled at her explaining away the details of the email communications and silently thought to myself, "Well, isn't that special." I kept quiet while she continued relaying the highlights and bullet points of who said what and how all the discussions got started. She emphasized the facts by increasing her tone, as if to say, you're not quite getting it here when I didn't become upset with all of the details.

"Mom, do you understand, it's too far to hike and carry enough food, water, and sleep gear for two days, and then go working in the hot sun. We can't do it, it's way too much for our age, and besides we need a break and some rest after all we have done in the Girl Scouts already." I kept nodding, smiling and listening when all of a sudden it hit me!

There it was in her dialog, "after all we have done in the Girl Scouts!" This was my answer to approach the subject with the girls next week at our meeting. I smiled, thanked and hugged her for sharing the information, and pulse of the group, by letting me know where everyone stood.

She was now on my heels, following me into the next room, "What are you going to do, Mom? Are you going to call them? Are you going to ask them about what I said was in the emails? What's going to happen now? Will you just tell me, so I know what's going to happen, or so I can tell them what you want to do?"

Again, I smiled and thanked her for getting me up to speed about their concerns and wishes, and assured her we would just talk about it during the meeting in the coming week. This made her notably nervous and uneasy, as she had now grown accustomed with family meetings in our house when I would silently prepare to address an issue. I am almost certain she followed up with the girls on emails, that I would probably be lecturing them when I arrived, and how I knew all about their discussions. Although she would never confirm it.

I prepared for the meeting by pulling out all of our past records, which I had thoroughly kept up to date for years. Glancing over all the stats and records made me feel tired also, and proud of them all in the same breath. I felt it too. We had done a lot over the years together, and now was not the time to lose the lesson by throwing on the brakes. This was a full throttle, Chuck Yeager, break through the sound barrier moment if ever there was one!

We needed to throw down the throttle here, and finish strong. I knew these girls, and their strengths and I knew they would never be satisfied with themselves finishing with a spa day and shopping spree. I understood the apprehensions, fears and a need for rest, but not when we were about to discover the sound barrier! It was pedal to the metal, go get the flag time, and don't come home with your tails tucked between your legs. We have to give this our best try, I reasoned to myself, because this is what we had been practicing for, building up to, learning and mentoring to one another for all these years! This is where the rubber meets the road, and I began tabulating and typing the results of all the years our troop had been in service together.

I compiled a list of their 63 greatest accomplishments in the last ten years of scouting and made copies. I made phone calls to each one of the parents that would be attending the meeting and briefly explained how our meeting would go. I asked them individually to grant me some time and leeway for addressing my concerns after I listened to the girls first. It was strategically important enlisting their cooperation, support, and silence, to gently guide the girls back to their own original goals and plans. Hopefully, in our silence, they would show some signs of being ready to take on the tasks, by figuring it out for themselves.

I further explained, "because if they don't come up with the answers, and the right answers, with some convictions about doing this project, then I would not be inclined to take them on a summit hike, under any conditions or circumstance." It was too risky, too dangerous, and life-threatening for them if they did not completely get on board, while understanding the commitments, being 100% sure, and responsible for their own decisions. Then after this one last plea, we would scrap the trip.

*

A week later, I flew over to Oahu, and we gathered at Danica's house for the meeting. There were hugs and greetings around, as it had been nearly four months since I'd seen them in person. After a warm up of banter and chatter, it was time to get down to business, and we called the meeting to order.

The girls seemed to shift with a somber disposition, just setting up the den with chairs. I asked them to put the seats in a theater style semi-circle of two rows. The parents paraded into the seats behind the first row, like a jury returning from a sequestered session, and left the girls looking at each other like, "What? You want us to sit in the front row?" I could feel the mood intoxicating the room like *I know she's going to give us a lecture.*

No one said a word as they filed in quietly and sat down. I waited until they were seated to sit on a chair in front of them, opening the meeting to them, saying "Okay girls, I understand you have some concerns about the trip, with specific laments about the hike and service project. Do you want to tell me what they are?" Then I stayed quiet to see who would go first.

There was dead silence for at least 2-3 minutes with everyone staring back and forth, and nobody leading the charge to address their position. I simply smiled back at them as if to say, *I have all the time in the world here, take all the time you need.* They stared back as if to say, *hurry up and give us our lecture so we can be done with this stupid meeting.* We all sat in our soundless stalemate until one brave soul decided to speak up.

Danica picked up the baton first, perhaps feeling the most comfortable in her own home, "Well Miss Pat, we have all been talking through the emails, and we don't think we are ready for that long of a hike, overnight for sure, carrying all the stuff on the list, and we decided we would like to do some other stuff instead."

After the iceberg had been tipped, they all wanted to jump in speaking, clamoring for the floor all at once. I waved my hands like a wand, trying to slow down the chatter, "I understand you all have something to add here, but I can't hear you all at once, we have plenty of time, let's take turns speaking, and we'll hear everybody's concerns."

They each spoke up addressing their concerns and misgivings, and we all listened intently for about thirty minutes, truly getting a point of view from everyone. I could see they had all really done their homework, and actually understood the complexities and difficulties of what we were about to embark on.

I could also see how they arrived at their uncertainties after completing so much of their research in my absence. I could certainly see how this happened, after watching Heather retreat in fear for the trial run, with me standing right next to her, supporting, encouraging and cheering her all the way to the trailhead. They were prepared, schooled, and ready for this challenging event, but were they over anxious from all the necessary ground work? Had I scared them to death with too much information? Into quitting altogether? We would know in a moment.

I knew they had to have all the knowledge of this mountain and her elements, even if they were over prepared, to ever consider taking this hike in such a dangerous location. This was a hike beginning at 10,000 feet, where the air is thin, the weather is unpredictable, and the elements are life-threatening. The desert conditions inside this extinct volcano crater can be unforgiving, with sun exposure, no water, and temperature fluctuations from freezing to heat exhaustion at a moment's notice. With no phones, phone service, and immediate emergency help, we had to be on it, to consider taking on this Goliath of a mountain! Yes, we had to have all the information!

I wasn't going to push too hard at this point, there was too much riding on the delicate line of being scared enough to protect themselves, and being prepared both mentally and physically to complete the hike without a hitch. They could not go in being naive about what to expect with regards to approaching and conquering this intensive course. My role now was to simply guide them to their own reality and conclusions of, "I'm ready, and I'm in," or "No, I'm not ready, and I'm out!"

After exhausting all their issues and concerns, I stood up to address them. Their body language slumped over chairs said, *here comes the lecture we've all been waiting for.* With arms defensively folded over their chests, some heads hanging off the backs of the seat rests, staring at the ceiling, while others stared off into space, a couple of girls glaring straight at me, I began passing out the typed list.

The parents seated quietly behind them, discreetly smirked, knowing somewhat the message about to be conveyed. I pretended not to notice anybody's demeanor in the room and kept right on passing out printed copies of their accomplishments. Once everyone had a copy, I walked back to the front of the room and began speaking sincerely and respectfully, to convey the way I genuinely felt.

I started off slowly and softly, hoping they were now ready to examine my message, in the spirit with which I wanted to transmit it. "Girls, we have been together as a troop for ten years now, and I have been your leader for nine of those years, and in all of that time we have learned and done many things together," I paused at each sentence to carefully choose the next, "Such as, learning to sign the Girl Scout Promise and the Law, and meeting our pen pal troop from the Big Island at council headquarters to greet and surprise them with it." I paused again, for each moment to take root and germinate a seed.

Then picking up the list in front of them and reading each line carefully, from the sixty-three entries of different subjects, projects or events we had done or experienced together, continuing, "We have marched, performed, attended, volunteered, participated, held, sponsored, toured, written, staffed, served, earned, completed, and achieved all sixty-three items on this list," reading them off one by one, with the number of times we did each subject, on each line, carefully letting it all sink in.

I paused for a moment, then finished with, "We have each earned nine Honor Troop pins, nine Aloha Ambassador badges, twenty-four Try-Its, thirty-six badges, ten Year pins, three Bridging badges, Brownie Wings, a WAGGAS World Girl Guide pin, a USA Girl Scout pin, a Program Aide badge, a Leadership pin, a Silver Award, earned and raised money for seven Cookie Blaster parties, with a record high sale in one year being the fourth highest in the state, donating to nine charities in ten cookie sales, and raising over $8,000 in three years for this project. And now you want to forego a 16-mile, overnight, backpacking service project trip that you have been preparing all these years for, to do a spa day, shopping trip, and sit at the beach?"

I sat down motionless, gazing at them, and waited for the response. They were expecting a lecture and probably still quietly wondering if it had just arrived. I didn't move, look away, gesture or flinch, I just sat there waiting for those germinating seeds to blossom into thriving plants. They started repositioning themselves, sitting up straighter in their chairs, looking down at the list, and back and forth at me. Their faces began to soften, as each one allowed the list they were staring at to sink in privately.

Chelsea decided to dust off the frost by doing something she would never have tried the first year of Brownies, speaking up first, with a hint of pride rising in her tone, "Wow, we did all of this?"

I responded gently, choosing my words judiciously, "Well you tell me, did you? Is there anything there that I made up or added, that we did not do together?"

The parents took up the full back row, cautiously biting their tongues. I could somehow feel their urgency to answer for them, and knew this discussion would go south quickly if we didn't allow them enough time to process and establish their own thoughts. This very moment was the sole reason I called each one discretely, to get us all in agreement, and on the same page. I knew we could not argue, lecture, reason, or try to give them our years of experience too quickly, by interrupting their contemplations.

I could feel these parents wanting to reach out, shake things up, and give them a wake-up nudge, however, they were collectively holding back, keeping with our agreement, letting each one of the girls go through their own process, arriving at their own conclusions, slowly and tediously, as it sometimes takes in youth.

The parents and I sat faithfully in standby mode, knowing the outcome could be victorious or disastrous, but it still all had to come from them. We couldn't walk this trail for them, and we couldn't make the decision either. I had to be 100% certain the decision came from them, and with some conviction, I might add!

Danica held up the list, waving it like a truce flag, slowly thawing out the chill devouring the room, "Well yeaaaah, we did do all of this, but it didn't seem like all that much until you look at it like this!"

I let her comment hang in the air to permeate the mood, while no one was taking a stand, in either direction.

Were they stunned by seeing it all laid out on paper? Were they waiting for more of a lecture? The muteness seemed to say a thousand things, yet nothing had been said at all.

While they may have been even a bit humbled by themselves, I began to speak again, slowly, with patience and ready for any outcome, "So you tell me, girls, is this the note you want to end your ten years of scouting on? Is this what you want to hang your hats on, and call it a day, bridging up to seniors with a shopping spree and a spa day?"

Silence befell the room again, and we could have heard a pin drop. This time, I waited them out, and no one wanted to point out the big white elephant sitting in the middle of the room. The only person within this dwelling who never had a quarrel with telling me off was Heather, so she started first, "Well you make it sound so bad if we do it that way."

Again, being careful with my content and not wanting to digress into a lecture, I reached for the best monotone sound I could muster and said, "I can't make anything sound so bad, or so good. Either you are proud to end on this note, or you are not? It really is your choice. I can't make it for you; I'm just your sounding board for what you guys have already been saying. That's all there is here; I'm just repeating your ideas."

We sat again in the frozen tundra of silence, letting them mull it over. Finally, the bravest and youngest soul by more than a year, Erin, spoke up in favor of the hike. She didn't have the deep roots of peer pressure like the other girls, who had been banded together since kindergarten, having only joined the troop at the end of our Juniors years. She bravely began, "Well, I'd like to try the hike, if anyone else would?"

Heather was the next to speak up supporting her, "Well I'll do it with you, Erin, it's really not that bad, I did it six months ago with my mom and dad, and it was kinda fun." I couldn't help but notice how strong the peer-pressure was here and how it kept her from exclaiming it was *really* fun, like when she talked non-stop to her dad and me, her teachers, friends, strangers and anyone else who would listen to all that she had learned, liked, and loved about her previous hike!

Danica was the next one to shift here and chimed in, "Well okay then, I'll go too, with you guys."

Chelsea was not one to ever back down from a physical challenge, and the next to jump on board, exclaiming, "Okay then, I'm in too!"

Kelcy was the last holdout, who was still perched with her arms folded across her chest. Everyone turned in her direction as if they had choreographed the movement, looking towards her at the exact same time for a response. With a blank look, she responded, "Whaaaaat? Why is everyone staring at me?"

All the girls rang her bell at the same time, "Come on Kelcy. You know what. Go with us. You can do this. We'll help you. We'll do it together. Come on!" These were a few of the comments I could decipher transmitting all at the same time. I couldn't tell who was saying what until Kelcy emerged the loudest bellowing, "Oh all right, I guess I'll go too," which quieted the troops.

However, it didn't sit well in my craw, and I had to intervene, "There is no guess here Yoda, either you are all the way in, or you are not? This hike is not an 'I guess' kind of commitment!"

I had witnessed Kelcy grow through the years, and undoubtedly come a long way with regards to hiking. However, this was different, the stakes were much higher now, and I wouldn't be able to push her to the limit on this particular adventure. No, this was an all-in venture, and it all had to come from her this time, with convictions coming from within.

She ho-hummed around for a few more tries, and finally spit out the correct verbiage that had some teeth in it, getting committed to run the gauntlet, but in the back of my mind, I was still somewhat worried about her initial hesitation. Also, factoring in that this wasn't her strongest suit, and she was under the gun of peer pressure when she arrived at her convictions, I would be keeping my hawk eye (pun intended) on her every step of the way, and I had to be certain she was ready to take on this very precarious next step.

For the rest of the meeting, we discussed the dynamics of all our pending travels, prep, and packing lists, and the service project in the delicate eco-system of the Haleakala National Park. With the last reminder about this adventure I reiterated, "We have to back-pack in everything we need, from bedding and shelter to food and water, and everything in between, and don't forget, if we pack it in, we have to pack it out."

Their purpose and excitement grew with the planning, challenges, and thrill of finally getting ready to earn our outdoor survival badge until Kelcy brought up the sore subject, and hard question, "Like what if we start our period, then what?"

Keeping it short and simple, I answered the question swiftly, moving on without a chance to feed the beast or lose the momentum, ending the subject on a positive note, "If we pack it in, we pack it out; it's the same answer for every question."

The room filled with groans and Kelcy rolled her eyes, "Oh, sweeeeet!" They all laughed at her sarcasm, and we swiftly moved on to the business of completing the last-minute paperwork for council. We had bigger fish to fry, with one more detail hanging over our heads. Our beloved Chrystal, Program Aide, mentor, and now great friend, who was hoping and planning to make this trip with us, was now on her way to college, with too many obligations coming her way to fulfill this one. As fate would have it again, the timing just didn't work out, and we still needed to replace her, with candidates and the window of time narrowing.

None of the other moms were signing up for this enterprise for sure, even though the dads were game, my husband was already signed up, as an additional adult. We simply had to have another female for the overnight emergency rule, in compliance with regulations on a Girl Scouting trip. Nevertheless, much like the way we had done most of our scouting tour through the years, we were still winging it with the final details and preparations. With all the paperwork filled out, signed, and ready to drop off at council, we left the meeting, ready to climb a mountain!

From here I could handle the remaining details via the phone, internet, and emails from Maui, and I took off for home. It seemed to be much easier now letting go and trusting that the universe would fix all the closing details that were beyond my reach. Lord knows I had all the details I could handle on the ground to oversee and I realized very early on in the planning stages that it was never within my control anyway. I put it out to prayers, and anyone who would listen, with solicitations for an athletic woman to fill our recent vacancy.

The door opened in time with an unlikely angel swooping in to rescue us, and willing to go on the hike. The news arrived during a discussion one day at church with a friend about our dilemma. She suggested her niece, who would be spending the summer with her in Maui after just completing high school. "She might be your candidate," she relayed, "not only eighteen but has some hiking experience as well."

My friend later confirmed with a phone call the uplifting news of hope we desperately needed to hear right away, that her niece Dakota was excited to get on board and take a hike with us!

CHAPTER 10
A WALK IN THE PARK

ITH ALL THE t's crossed, and all the i's dotted, we were in the final preparations for our long-awaited, inner-island trip. In the few days leading up to their arrival on Maui, the email responses were highly encouraging, and the thrust was building right up to, and including, getting on the plane. I was pleasantly surprised and even optimistic about how excited Kelcy was getting over doing the hike and service project.

Houston, we are ready for takeoff!

The girls called from the airport on Oahu as soon as everyone checked in, and the anticipation was mounting. Heather, her dad and I were waiting in the wings with two cars to pick them up from Kahului airport, arriving on a 1:00pm flight. Excitement was in the air, and so were the girls!

The minute they walked onto the curb in Maui, it was a fully vested pajama party with squeals, screams, and giggles, just like the old days! They were amped up for this seven-day event with the same enthusiasm as the first kindergarten gathering. As much as things had changed, ten years later they were still the same!

They each arrived with a suitcase and a twenty-five-pound backpack ready to go for the survival hike scheduled on the following morning. The week prior to their arrival, I purchased and prepared all the provisions including food and water for the trip. All we had on the schedule for the first day, besides traveling from Oahu, was a fun and easy craft project, getting food and water into the backpacks, and double checking their survival gear. Then it was downtime, relaxation, catching up and socializing of course.

Heather's bedroom became the catch-all, makeshift closet for suitcases, handbags, and backpacks. The living room of our two-bedroom condo doubled as the slumber room, gathering air mattresses, sheets, blankets, and pillows, filling every crevice of space. As soon as we landed at the apartment, they winged their gear on the bedroom floor, and they were off again exploring the beach across the street. The clock was ticking with too much to see and too little time to do it all. The adrenaline kept them on the move and completely wound up. I was all too happy to see them on the go and excited again.

My friend from church and her niece Dakota arrived with hiking gear while the girls were out sightseeing and I was setting up for their craft activity and dinner. We got better acquainted, chatting while they helped me with the setup. The final craft project would also be a gift from me, and they would be making glitzy, rhinestone slippers, which sold at all the top spas for a mere $200 a pair. I purchased the rubber slippers in a multitude of styles, sizes, and colors leaving on the tags for a return, after selections and fittings were made, along with waterproof glue and dozens of colored stones.

Second on the craftsmanship agenda, I located a box full of old photos holding ten years of memories and purchased scrapbooks and materials for each girl to personalize with her favorite photos of troop adventures. Yes, the final gathering would have to include our traditional craft artistries in tribute of troop meetings, while doubling as a closing keepsake gift from maw.

The girls began straggling in from the beach, meeting Dakota one or two at a time, and delving into their slippers projects, which required several days for drying time. Using their unique talents, each one was exceptionally crafted with some gorgeous color schemes and patterns, making every distinct one much like their designers, a treasured gem.

Also, part of our tradition in scouting was the launching of get-togethers with a dinner party in true Hawaiian style. Moving the festivities outside to a cozy enclosure adjacent to the living room, in a garden courtyard, summoned in a local ambiance surrounded by tropical growth, with palm trees and obscure lighting amongst the flora. Tikki torches sprinkled the indigenous atmosphere while delicately illuminated lanterns breathed air into the native celebration.

The customary barbecue marked the opening of our week filled with adventures, and once again I slowed down the view as if watching the movie from afar. I wanted to encompass it all, and capture these moments on a video or in a photo, yet somehow I couldn't pull myself away from the banter and merriment to grab a camera. Nor could I stop etching these portraits, drawing them within my mind.

I participated, engaging with everyone while simultaneously observing the fête of perfect balance like it was an overview from outside the gathering itself. Perceiving the moments in which the culminating dashes of life were the beginning and ending of an era and gazing at the elusive patio lighting, noticing the laughter, giggling, mingling and socializing with joy and sadness, I tried to stay in the present moments of our sunset celebration.

Also true to form, it took effort shutting down our scouting festivities of talking story, reminiscing about the adventures of our past, and catching up on current events. However, we had the main event awaiting at daybreak, and cleanup and bathroom chores to perform before bedtime. Housing only one bathroom, this was going to be a feat in and of itself.

Forging ahead in the schedule, we slowly wound down the day with everyone staking out a claim in the wall-to-wall chambers of the living room, after lavatory shifts. Once everyone landed, I nestled into the middle of the disheveled space on a recliner with my ever-famous checklist, cases of water and stacks of rations earmarked for sorting into backpacks. This was our final check-in for completing preparations on our sunrise mountain ascent.

Everyone had packs seated beside them for the ritual of getting everyone on the same page. I read down the supply list while they located each item in their backpacks, countering in a roll call fashion to check it off the list. Once all items were accounted for, I tossed out the rations of food and water to be incorporated into the gear. With the final task of the day completed, my husband collected the bags and stored them away in our cars for a quick getaway in the morning.

The final debriefing included safety reminders, time schedules, and some strict guidelines about sunscreen and hydration, with a reminder that I, yes maw, would absolutely be monitoring proper water intake and sunscreen applications on an hourly basis. They were so wired-up and excited I wasn't even sure they heard me at this juncture.

It was a typical slumber party on steroids with horsing around, playing, joking, laughing and teasing, girly girl style. I couldn't believe my eyes! Were these the same girls I met with a couple of weeks ago on Oahu? The ones who were all, "Don't look at me, I don't wanna hike 'cause it's too far, and it'll be too hard." They were polar opposites now, bouncing off the walls, screaming with laughter, and havin' a ball!

I was relieved to see them so excited, knowing it would take every bit of energy they could muster to thrust them up a mountain, however, I was still keeping my fingers crossed that it would

last. The way I had it figured, if we got through the mountain project first, the rest of the week would be a walk in the park, at least
this was my mantra while hoping my momentum lasted all week
as well.

It was all going so smoothly thus far, and I couldn't believe
my luck, or was it just the adrenaline? They didn't even complain
when I dispersed the eight 16oz bottles of water adding consider-
able weight to their packs. It was like they never even noticed, or
was it all the preparation and homework that deflated the natural
facts and effects of the heaviness? Either way, I was relieved to be
through this hurdle, and ready to wind it down for slumber.

They were still situating, tossing and turning when I flipped
out the lights at 10:00pm, and this certainly wasn't the end of the
pajama party rompings in their hyper state of excitement. The
high energy would be helpful at the crack of dawn for getting our
engines started, however, not so effective for shutting down quickly
or getting to sleep. This took several reminders, just like the good
old days, to squelch the constant talking, giggling and squirming.

The moment they reached la-la land and silence befell the
house, I lay awake in contemplation of the days to come. Staring
out a window lured by the translucent light of the stars, I felt calm,
ready and self-assured that we had everything in place, and we were
ready for leaping into this next step of the journey.

Then suddenly without notice, the warning bells started going
off with concepts mixed in fears. They snuck through the backdoor
of my psyche, creeping their way into my being, probing with the
endless questions about the impending project just ahead.

Things like, *Are you really up for this task?* And, *can you really
handle sixteen miles into the wilderness, defying all the elements, toting
thirty pounds of gear, while getting them all out safely? Dear God what
have you gotten yourself into again?* Finally, going down the rabbit
hole with, *what if this happens, and what if that happens?* All these

scenarios started playing out a concert in my head, waiting for the maestro to wave a magic wand, and put an end to their chronicles.

However, before the full crescendo, there was a finale performance with questions about the questions, like, *why do I still have these moments of self-doubt? I thought I handled most of my self-doubts already, so where do they keep coming from, and why do they come up at all? Do they actually have a purpose? Is it simply for normal checks and balances? Is it to keep me safe or alert, and on my toes? Is it perhaps just a default mechanism, making me aware of any and all problems or possible dangers that can occur? What is it, and am I totally the only one who ever has these questions, fears, and doubts coming up in my head?*

I did make some profound and pertinent decisions about all the discussions rambling around in my head. For the most part, these contemplations revealed good news in that I don't let these doubts and fears stop me dead in my tracks any longer. This was a huge step in the right direction, versus the past, where at least I get past these thoughts now, and I run from them. They don't run me anymore! Yes, these were my strides and revelations in this arena alone where I found growth. I only carried a small billy club now, instead of the proverbial 2x4 I used to swing to drive away the nagging tentacles of fear, worry, and doubt.

It would be nice if these thoughts would just move out of my head completely, however, just in case there's a purpose for having them, I skimmed the final checklist one more time. With much ado over nothing, I gladly turned it all over to a higher authority in the universe asking for protection and blessings to carry us all on this next step of our voyage into the unknown.

*

We started the next day in the usual hustle and bustle rush with a single bathroom. Getting on the road before the crack of dawn, we drove about an hour before daylight around the island and up the mountain to arrive at Haleakala National Park Headquarters as soon as it opened. At the park's entrance, we obtained outdoor camping and hiking permits, along with rules and regulations for the park, and watched a training film with education about the summits delicate eco-system.

I met with a park ranger about our service project while the girls were set up with the video. She asked if we would be interested in doing an extra service project while at our campsite the next morning, further explaining they were in the process of making a new training film for the park services. We both glanced over at the girls viewing the antiquated film, agreeing with just a nod and smile; it was past due.

They could have a photographer up at our campsite location in the morning to take some current photos of the girls in their subject matter if we were interested in participating. She also advised there was no assurance they would actually use the photos in the training video. It would not be her, the photographer, or anyone in their local office putting the final work together. We would simply participate in the photo shoot, sign a waiver for submitting the shots, and find out later if we made the cut when the film was completed.

She felt the scouts had a good chance of being part of the examples they were looking for, because they usually had all the proper gear, and followed park rules very closely. We decided it would reasonably fit into our current schedule. Agreeing on a meeting time, we completed our tasks at the headquarters and set our sights for the summit which was another 20-30 minute drive up the slopes.

The weather was reigning smiles on us from the jump of the day, with temperatures in the low 50s. Truly a blessing for this mid-June day, considering the possibilities we had just witnessed on the training video. The film articulated how we could experience anything from grueling hot to freezing cold conditions at a moment's notice. Rain, storms, hail and high winds could blow in at any time of year, changing and affecting wind chill factors and temperatures at this altitude. We were certainly prepared for it all but were relieved to have mild, slight winds, no rain, and a flawless sunshiny day to launch the expedition.

We transported everyone to the summit, unloading all the gear, hydrating, applying sunscreen, layering clothing and making final lavatory runs while my husband made the scramble 3,000 feet back down the mountain leaving a car in the lower parking lot loaded with snacks and water. The plan on the second day included hiking out of the crater on the switchback trail near the car. We all rendezvous by 9:00am at the designated starting point known as the Sliding Sands Trail.

The famous trail drops into a picturesque, colorful desert of swirling lava formations. The bowl-shaped depression looks like Mother Nature used an ice cream scooper to carve out a ten mile wide 4,000-foot deep cavity into the dormant volcano's cone. We started our hiking experience with a group photo at the trailhead's classic view, and one of the world's most magnificent masterpieces.

The apex of grandeur lays out miles of the park's natural beauty and wonders in one breadth. The barren canvas floor is dotted with a maze of smaller black cinder cones protruding from the desolate landscape. The early morning sun accentuated and enhanced the variations of color, illuminating yellows, oranges, and reddish brown hues swirling and churning against the sharp contrast of black volcano dust. The jagged perimeter peaks dusted with greenery set against a deep blue skyline depicted a postcard glimpse of the treasures to come.

With everyone situated, we pulled on our thirty-pound packs stepping into our futures on this ominous trail. The big adventure began here, and we were ready to embrace all the majesty this mountain creation had to offer. The girls led the pack in a single file march on the narrow pathways, with my husband and I bringing up the rear flanks. The moving sounds of crushing lava embers beneath our boots seemed magnified in the undisturbed silence.

Each purchasing step gave way like quicksand, which further pro-pelled us down the crag in corresponding harmony with the trail's namesake Sliding Sands.

I soon began to appreciate how many more silver swords were growing and multiplying along the trail. Remembering my first visit to this mountain nearly twenty years earlier, I could picture my old photos with the barren landscape when these rare and sensitive flow-ers were almost extinct. The endangered native plant was now flourishing with fences in place completely surrounding the park, whereby removing the goats which were feasting on the delicate snack. Coupled with the efforts of volunteer workers eradicating invasive weeds, which were also choking out the flowing shrubs, these unusual blossoms on a thirty-year reproduction cycle were making a healthy comeback now gracing and beautifying the trails with impressive numbers.

Haleakala, which means *house of the sun*, holds the rare distinc-tion of being the only National Park in our country enclosed by a fence. With much accreditation going out to the Maui community of volunteers for their love and dedication helping with the comple-tion of such a feat. This amazing mountain, rich and full of history, character, and chi is all-enduring, holding many mystical qualities. It seemed serendipitous for us to be spending our last hurrah shar-ing her magnificence and sanctions together.

I metaphorically reflected that taking on the challenges of this troop have been at times my biggest mountain to climb in life, and now we were all at the top of the world climbing a mountain together. Just seeing the girls walking down the mountain trail con-jured up a tidal wave of memories, and I began wavering back and forth from nostalgia into the present.

I felt a sense of pride observing the flashbacks popping in and out of my memories, and I could still see them plain as day, tooth-less giggling Brownies on our very first hike together. The visualiza-tions conjured up sounds and images as if I were presently in these moments. I pictured them rambling down a lush tropical trail on a ridge near my home to find a glimpse of the ocean. The Sacred Garden Trail was stretching our limits, walking three-quarters of a mile to the gazebo perched in the middle of the path. We snapped a photo of them all wearing their glittery, Valentine t-shirts, personally crafted and designed the week before our maiden hike, which later became the signature print for their troop scrapbook. They were all a sight, full of energy and love for life. My heart swelled watching them with endearment and appreciation, which continually expanded my world and characteristics. I somehow discovered along the way that most of my character actually developed by having them following me. Every time they struggled, whined, complained, or hit their walls, I had to step it up and grow a little more with them as if we lifted one another up simultaneously on the roads we traveled together.

Much like a mother forgets the pains of labor moments after giving birth, all the lessons we shared with difficulty, adversity, resistance and mood swings were now fading into the farthest recesses of my mind, bringing forth the growth and wisdom we inevitably obtained. I was grappling to let it all seep in slowly, taking long, deep yoga breaths to control my heart rate which seemed to be racing faster than usual. As if breathing were no longer an involuntary action, I had to keep reminding myself just to take deep breaths, keep taking deep breaths. I rationalized that it must be the emotional connections, along with the high altitude and thin air.

To say the very least, this hike was climactic, witnessing life's progressions on the fly, walking along the trail behind these young ladies. They were emerging from little girls before my very eyes in a framework of events while I reproduced each moment from the past within my thoughts. Moment by moment I embraced the joy, laughter, humor, excitement, gratification, honor and self-esteem we all cultivated out of the paths we ultimately chose together.

Recalling all we had gone through bringing us to this place, at just this moment in a speck of time, my thoughts echoed in the eerie silence of the hollow canyon walls. This all-encompassing moment engulfed everything from the minute I said, "I'll be your leader for a year, and we'll see how things go later," until this very instant on our descent into the crater. These extraordinary events scrolled across a screen in my head, recounting gifts and blessings I most certainly received along the way.

My thoughts shifted into calculating how much I had learned and grown in spite of my own doubts and misgivings. Without question, I learned about leadership and summoning these qualities from within, which were always there latent and resting, with nowhere else to go except, like cream, rising to the top for every single occasion. I learned about giving to others in such a profound way. However, more importantly, I learned that through these acts of giving, I received so much more than I gave. I experienced commitment, not only by becoming committed but also by knowing all the amazing individuals I came across and worked with along the path.

These startling awarenesses were powerful, yet humbling discoveries, bringing with them a mixed bag of emotions swelling into tears and smiles all in the same notions. I remembered all the sacrifices everyone displayed, in every act of kindness issued on this journey. I felt all the immeasurable rewards I received by simply accepting the ride they asked me to hitchhike on with them. Yes, they were major contributors to most of my character development and were yet again taking me on another jaunt, schooling me infinitely about the most important things in life.

I didn't want to register yet how this would be our last and final hike together as a troop. These petrifying thoughts stayed in the back of my mind while I continued compiling the substantial lists of experiences, lessons, honors and memories positively carrying me down the inclines.

*

The first mile was a lifetime journey for me anyway and went by in a flash. With the girls still upbeat and excited, we took our first break on a cliff to rest and breathe in the views. On these one-mile intervals, we reapplied sunscreen, explored the surrounding areas, shared snacks and checked in with everyone's needs, which was a part of keeping with our plans to stop and smell the roses while enjoying the journey on a hike.

We descended several thousand feet with each mile, which meant the temperature was rising quickly. Carrying our heaviest rations of water and food at this point meant we truly needed our one-mile breaks for proper hydration and keeping a steady pace. The goal of reaching our lunch destination at around the six-mile marker would put us at the Kapalaoa cabin pretty much in the center of the valley.

The first two stops went well, and the views were incredible, but everyone was beginning to tire a bit by the end of the third mile. They kept a stiff upper lip about the fatigue on the third break and pushed forward and downward towards the desert flats at approximately the 6500-foot level. Reaching the abyss of this volcano ash ravine and cinder cone valleys which cut off the gentle breezes and coupled with the rapid elevation drop and the mercury rapidly rising, needless to say with thirty-pound backpacks, our internal heat rose as well.

The temperature was almost 80 degrees at the four-mile marker with absolutely no shade, and the girls began thrusting down backpacks and collapsing on top of them with body language that said *we're done*! Danica and Kelcy were approaching me while I was pulling off my pack. Using a tone that said listen up here, they began with, "Ms. Pat, all of us want to talk with you before we go any further."

"Okay, what's up?" I inquired as the entire posse of girls surrounded me like a swarm of bees.

Heather, the imperishable spokeswoman for the troop, spoke up boldly, "We have all talked about it, and we don't want to go on another six miles today in this heat, and another six miles tomorrow.

This is awful, we're hurting, we're carrying too much weight, we're too hot, and we're all too tired to keep going this way. We want to go back up the way we just came down, and go home right now. We're done with this hike."

I took a deep breath needing to cool down myself and calmly replied, "Okay girls, go to the bathroom if you need to, get a snack and some water, reapply sunscreen, and we'll all have a meeting in ten minutes after I have a breather and a break too."

If looks could kill, I would have dropped on the spot, and we had us a full-on troop mutiny going again! They were kicking the dirt and scattering like mice in all directions. From their distance, they continued glaring at me with nowhere on the torrid terrain to find shade or relief. My husband, being the silent leader of this all-female group, arrived just in time to catch the tail end of our discussion. While pulling off his forty pounds of weight and grief, he inquired with a sense of urgency, "What's going on here?"

"Well it seems they have run out of gas a little early on this trip, and they want to turn around and go back out the way we just came down, right now!"

"What did you tell them?" He continued the conversation in a lowered voice out of their earshot.

"I told them we would be having a meeting in ten minutes after they've had some rest and refreshments, and I've had a breather with some time to think."

He began shaking his head grinning and wiping the sweat from his balding forehead in his ever-famous front to back motion with a bandana saying, "You're not actually thinking of taking them any further then? Are you?"

Both of us began staring back and forth in a long pause, clearly at a standoff. I broke the silence first, "We'll see in ten minutes. I need to recover for a few minutes and think about it first."

I stepped away to recoup, and he stayed right on my heels, trying to steer my thoughts getting his vote in early, "I don't want to go another foot with these girls if they're not into it for themselves. It's a desert out there, and we can't get them back if they give up half way. I say we turn around right now. I can't help you or get them out of this if it turns bad out there. I'm carrying all the weight that I can handle for myself right now, so you need to listen to what they are saying to you right now."

I was still moving away from him, and he kept speaking, "Are you listening to me? Are you listening to them?" he continued.

I turned around putting my hand up for a gesture of silence, hoping to pause our communication. After a long deep breath, I slowly responded, "Like I said, we all need a ten-minute break, and I need to think first."

He shook his head again with a chuckle, giving me one of those *here we go* looks, which didn't require words after many years of marriage. "Don't give me that look right now, just give me a break," I pleaded, walking away to meditate.

Ten minutes had a way of giving me a new perspective, however, not so much for the disposition of my partner or the girls. They were sitting or lying on backpacks scattered around a bush that resembled a tumbleweed when I walked up to address them. My husband stood behind me leaning on the wooden hitching post used for tying up the horses from the riding tours. The scene reminded me of an old western where the sheriff comes riding into town, and the posse wants a new man to wear the town's badge.

I really wanted to start out with humor like, "Okay gals, I understand you and the posse have had a town meetin', and you need a new sheriff." However, I wisely decided against it, thinking they didn't seem like they could handle humor at this very moment in time. Instead, I reached for words of wisdom, even though I truly wanted to ask the creator to snatch them back before I spoke them aloud.

I leaped in soliciting my angels to get my back and somehow create a miracle because I needed all the support I could get standing in this lonely place of leadership, now facing down a lynch mob. I began to speak without a clue of how it would all play out in the end, winging it so to speak, again! "So girls, I get that you're all feeling overwhelmed and tired at this point, that is very understandable; however, I hope you're all feeling a little better after some food, water, and rest."

Ignoring the scowling looks, foot tapping, arms crossed and blatant stares I continued, "We are not even at the halfway point of this hike, and I can see how you might think it is better to go back right now from here, but the reality is this, (pointing towards the summit from which we just came) it's nearly a 4,000-foot climb in that direction to the car, which is all up hill on sliding black sand cinders. In this heat with full packs, it is *not* a good idea or a good plan. Or we can go in that direction (pointing towards the cabin and the center of the valley) two miles on a solid flat surface to eat some lunch and rest for an hour. We'll be well over the half-way point for the day, our packs will keep getting lighter, and it will cool off by the time we reach our campsite for setup, where we can rest for the night. Tomorrow our packs will be even lighter, and the climb out will be on a firm rock ground with even milder temperatures in the south basin."

No one jumped for joy, in fact, no one moved at all. I was the only one reaching for my backpack, putting it on while continuing to speak, "Now we can take on this hike one mile at a time, stopping every half hour for food, water, and rest, assessing where everybody is at, or we can take it all on sixteen miles at once in your heads. That is what you guys are doing right now. You're getting yourselves overwhelmed because you're over thinking it. You're trying to do it all at once in your heads. We need to let all of that go right now, and let's do this hike one mile at a time, then we'll check in and see where you are from there."

I began buckling up my pack while they hadn't moved an inch, in fact, no one even flinched. They were all staring me down like *go ahead, try to make us move right now*, and we definitely had ourselves a full standoff! About to walk away I spoke my last bit of advice, "and if you are physically unable to stand, walk or move one more inch, after the next mile, I will personally find a park ranger with a horse to haul you out of here. So, if I can walk one more mile at fifty years old, I'm thinking you girls can handle it at fourteen and fifteen. Otherwise, I'll check in with you at the next mile marker to see who's still standing or not."

I turned walking towards the path, and Chelsea was the first one to her feet. Pulling on her pack, she caught up to me inquiring, "Yoouuurrr fifty?" I nodded, and she sped away muttering, "I'm not letting any fifty-year-old out hike me."

The rest took her lead and followed suit trying to catch up, giving me stink eye on the pass with their best drive by looks. My husband and I were left in the rear flanks again to walk in silence while I caught a few more disapproving stares from him, which I promptly and wisely ignored as well.

After a few minutes, Erin, the youngest of our collective, fell back and walked at my side. She began confessing that she was really glad we weren't turning back, but she didn't want to stand out and go against the rest of the girls. She also confirmed she was in as much pain as the others, but she was really proud of herself for doing this hike and service project. I assured her the other girls would feel the same way very soon, and praised her for being mature beyond her years, being able to see past the physical pain, and already looking at the bigger picture.

A few minutes later, my daughter Heather dropped back to walk with Erin and I, complaining the other girls were talking stink about me, and she didn't want to hear it anymore. She could do it anytime she wanted; however, it was different if others did. Again, I assured them both that "this too shall pass," reminding them both that we get a chance to see who we really are in times of pain and challenges when we hit our proverbial walls. This is where we grow, and without a challenge we would never make advances or progress beyond our adolescent experiences in life.

Then Erin changed the subject by asking, "Ms. Pat, what did you mean when you said we were doing the whole sixteen miles in our heads, instead of one mile at a time?"

I thought about it for a moment and decided to answer her question with a question, for possibly drawing out the profound thoughts with her deciphering the statement for herself. "Well, let me ask you this, do you ever swim in the ocean?"

She replied slowly, "Yeeeesss?" with a high pitch tone at the end as if to ask *where is this going, and how does it apply to walking in a desert?*

"Well, have you ever swam against the tide, or with it?"

Again, in confusion, she replied, "Yes, but what does that have to do with this hike?"

Staying with our theme, I asked, "Well, what happens when you swim with the tide?"

She perked right up, "It's much easier, and you will go further and much faster."

I continued, "Then what happens when you swim against the tide?"

She was getting the drift, "It's a lot harder, and you have to work twice as hard to go half as fast, soooo I still don't see what this means walking on a hike."

Now we had a foundation to work with, and I began with the analogy, "Well, when you are thinking about hiking a long distance of sixteen miles in two days, it's just like swimming with or against the tide in the ocean, and it all starts in your head first. If you're over thinking it too much, like 'this is going to be so hard' or 'we have too far to go,' then you're focusing all about the entire sixteen miles ahead with every step, and this can weigh you down, that's when you're thinking about the whole thing all at once. This is much like swimming against the tide in the ocean."

Checking in to see if she was following, "Do you see what I'm trying to say?" Heather was showing interest now, and they both began nodding yes. I continued "Now if you train yourself to think in terms of one step at a time, enjoying the views along the path, and you start thinking, 'I only have to walk one mile then I can rest,' you're only taking on that small section in your mind. You break it down only doing what is right in front of you. That is like swimming with the tide in the ocean. Does this make any sense?"

"Yes, it does!" Both girls chimed in, and the light bulb was finally clicking on! I elaborated a bit more, "So don't think about the entire hike, or even take on the next mile in your thoughts, until after you have rested both your body and your mind covering only the mile right front of you. What you'll find is that you will actually enjoy each moment you are in more, the miles and the hike will go much faster with a lot less effort, like swimming with the tide instead of against it. Do you think you can try this?"

They both nodded in agreement. We continued the discussion by adding on the benefits of relaying this thinking process to a group or collective of people such as ours. Conveying that one negative thought or attitude in a group will infect, or affect the entire group with a direction or result, impacting everyone much in the same way an individual thought process will affect you.

I then used the example of why they wanted to peel off from the disgruntled group discussion because it weighed them down. Erin picked up the baton first and ran with it, "So if the group has the same positive attitude and mindset, the thinking will also change the tide for everyone in the group as well?"

And voilà... Houston, we have made contact!

I loved how easily they were connecting all the dots, and I replied quickly, "Yes, either in a good way or bad way, but it's all a choice, and it all starts in our heads, with our thinking, which we control if we want to, then it transfers to our attitudes, and our behaviors, which finally affects our results, again either in a good way or a bad way. However, it's still our choice. So girls, what do you want to choose today, right now; to go with the tide, or against it? It's just a matter of deciding!"

They both shared their thoughts admitting they weren't feeling so overwhelmed anymore, and they were actually starting to feel more comfortable, even relaxed, just talking about it. They were also pleasantly surprised to discover we had just walked nearly a mile during our chat, without even realizing it. With their new-found beliefs, they wanted to speed up and catch the other girls, deciding it would be helpful to explain this novel theory and let them know it was time for a one-mile marker break.

As the girls marched off to explain their innovative new philosophies with their cohorts, my husband gave me another sideways look and a smirk. The kind where we communicated without using any words, while shaking his head and laughing.

"What does that mean?" I questioned. And he knew exactly what I meant, without an explanation.

"How long do you think that positive attitude speech is going to hold up in this heat?"

"At least two days I hope," and we both burst into laughter at the implications, then gasping for air with all the weight we were shouldering in the heat! We walked the last mile before lunch, peacefully enjoying the sounds of solicitude. This pristine aura captured my attention on our first voyage into the summit, and it was now unfolding as my favorite place on earth.

Reaching our sixth mile marker close to 1:00pm, we were in the range of staying on our tentative schedule. The girls were more than a sight for sore eyes frolicking around the cabin, shoes off, lounging in the grass, socializing with the Nene geese, and truly looking like they had adopted a new attitude.

Erin was notably excited to see me, rushing over while my pack was diving to the ground. "Miss Pat," she began with excitement like you've gotta hear this! "We have decided to give our hike a name, and we're going to call it 'Going With the Flow,' so it reminds us to swim with the tide, instead of against it. Isn't that a cool name for it?"

Pulling my boots and socks off for a personal foot massage, I smiled outwardly and silently affirmed inward, "I knew these girls had it in them, we just had to dig a little deeper to find it."

"Very cool indeed Erin, I like it. Every hike at the summit needs a name, and that one is very clever and appropriate. I do like it very much!"

Laying back to rest my eyes and soak up the vitamin D, I smiled again thinking, "we're back in the game, and hopefully this high tide will float us all the way to the shoreline with *ten* miles to go!"

CHAPTER 11

IT'S A MOUNTAIN TOP EXPERIENCE

THE LUNCH BREAK was the quickest hour of the day where we seemed to mend a lot of the fences. Starting the next jaunt of our journey meant biting off the last three-and-a-half miles on the daily itinerary. With fresh outlooks, rest, food, hydration, and their newly remodeled upbeat signature theme, I was now the one having trouble keeping up with them.

They began marching again in a single file line with reverence for the narrow pathways, this time singing familiar scout songs. I couldn't help but smile, desperately fighting back the urge to chuckle right out loud. I couldn't get the vision of the seven dwarfs out of my head, and the humorous parallel it was creating. Needless to say, their hiking melodies and my funny bone, carried us all the way through the last leg of the day without a hitch.

They were finally taking pleasure in the journey, instead of letting the journey take their pleasure away. Without their gray matters getting in the way, they actually began drinking in all the marvels this unspoiled mountaintop could display. We began sharing the ride and bonding around the perpetually changing scenery, amazing colors, and fluctuating terrains, with each mile escorting in new sites and shifting weather conditions the summit is famous for. One minute it felt like we were walking on the moon, and then like hiking into the Grand Canyon, or the next moment the Mohave Desert.

The rapidly changing ecosystems in the Hawaiian mountains hold a unique distinction, producing climates of rainforest, subalpine, shrublands, deserts and cloud forest all within a matter of hours and or miles. We took it all in, hiking nearly ten miles on the first day. By the time we dropped our heavy knapsacks on the west basin ridge to set up camp, we were all pretty happy hikers. Tents went up quickly, and excitement was back in the air at our new destination.

The girls clamored off to explore the area with energy to burn after fortifying with a light dinner while I settled down to breathe in the moments. Perched on a plush carpet of grass I closed my eyes to feel the mountain's mystique that is unlike any place I have ever experienced on earth. The massive 4000-foot ridges protrude from the plush green valley floors encompassing and encasing the basin depression in 360 degrees of panoramic beauty. This impeccable alcove creates a niche towards the heavens with a natural sound barrier from the demanding clamor of civilization below.

The elevation magnifies every minuscule sound like the humming vocals of a fly buzzing on a blade of grass. To a breeze amplifying whispers which ripple like a wave across the tufts of wild greenery. I paused within the stillness, engaging all my senses, and could actually detect the earth's massive vibration beneath the roaring sounds of thunderous quiet. This reverberation seemed to have a monumental force which resonated into every cell of my body, penetrating its life force deep within my bones, balancing out every last tissue into a perfect pitch of harmony. This is energy I thought, Nirvana!

As if I were one with the planet, I experienced the rhythmic movements and authoritative commands in equally valued proportions to my own natural functions. On this epic ride I could feel the earth's tundra emerging from its rotation with an esoteric sound like a roaring vortex, awakening all my senses to new levels of understanding, echoing from within these movements, heralding to my soul, and conveying with all its thrust, welcome to the globe, welcome to the universe, and welcome to your life!

As if I had performed a chiropractic enlightenment adjustment within my own mindset, the messages resonated affirming, *all you need in life is commissioned from within, abundantly available throughout the universe, and transferrable to all you touch upon the earth.* The messages were loud and clear, and all I had to do to simply tap into them was shut out all the noise and chaos, with all the distractions, demands, and self-imposed stress long enough to hear them, long enough to believe it.

Unassumingly conveyed and confirmed by simply connecting with my roots, our mother earth, and finding a state of bliss apprehended from within, a state which truly exists by tuning in and listening, not constructed of any hocus-pocus, loud music, potions, pills, or drugs, but everything at my own disposal right inside. Using only what I arrived upon this earth with, sanctioned for the asking, whenever I want to tap into it.

My humorous side kicked in remembering a cartoon I received from a single mom while teaching a parenting class. Pictured was a guru with a long beard in flowing robes, perched high atop a mountain sitting in the lotus position with a man, tattered and worn, kneeling at his feet asking, "Teacher, what is the meaning of life?" The guru answers, "The meaning of life is listening to what your mother has been telling you all along; now go home, and stop climbing these silly mountains." So it all comes down to simple answers, and as much as we or I want to confound things, it really doesn't need to be complicated. It comes right down to getting back to basics.

I breathed in these simple pleasures, relaxing with the surroundings, and basking in the stillness when the girls wandered over and sat down quietly in my vicinity taking in the spectacular views. The scenery at dusk had become so vividly clear it felt like you could virtually reach out and touch each rock or curvature with your perceptions, akin to watching a 3D movie. The glowing sunset augmented every detail of the canyon walls with startling clarity, like a spotlight on every crevice reigning in the fine points.

The gradual dawning color ignited the sky, blending fluorescent mixtures of yellow, orange, and crimson while fading into a light blue dome overhead, and a deep aquatic blue on the opposite side of the canopy. The jagged mountain ridges drew their own distinctive lines silhouetted against the rainbow ceiling of hues, with their own synthesizing shades of swirling yellowish browns, blacks, gold and greens mingling into new fusions of pigment.

A medley of stars fashioned their way onto the vastness of this canvas long before a prevailing darkness in a breathtaking overture from the universe like none I'd ever seen before. On the screen of the next opus, a nearly full moon crested from behind the rugged cliffs, bursting forth like a brilliant star appearing closer in the illusion than it actually was, hailing skyward in its own pace.

White clouds billowed in covering the summit floor just below our perch, lending to the vibe like we were sitting at the edge of heaven, looking down upon the earth. We sat motionless, in awe, watching all the universe zoom into these peaks with a spectacular performance delivered by the cosmos.

In the deafening stillness, nature struck another poetic cord with a recital from the Ua'u birds tooting their mating calls. These rare birds only serenade at night and are not found anywhere else on earth except in the Hawaiian Islands at these elevations. Their acoustical pitch echoed off the canyon walls, sounding much like a flute, fluttering from an ancient cultural instrument. Vibrating the entire valley with Mother Nature's operetta, accompanied by the rhythm of my own heartbeat and breath, the resounding narration raised every hair on my body, permeating every one of my senses.

This place radiates enchantment, and the girls seemed to know it without the need to communicate a single word. I could feel their endearment, watching them draped and leaning on one another, mouth's gaping open, enraptured by the miracles unfolding at their feet. Their smiles said it all, unspoken yet in a thousand words marveling at these landscapes swathed in and by God's grace and beauty. From time to time our eyes met for a brief look or glance, and they seemed to be saying *thank you*, with a momentary expression.

I perceived their accomplishment with a mere gaze that seemed to be saying thank you and so much more like, *thank you for pushing us through all our little girl crap in order to bring us to this place, this place of magic and wonder, of calmness and magnificence. Thank you for not letting us give up on ourselves, or go crying back to the car with our tails tucked.* Yes, they had all of this and more written across their faces, conveyed in silent appreciation simply sitting in serenity high atop a mountain.

We were at a pinnacle of our scouting adventures together, and I could absolutely feel them turning a corner, even if they didn't recognize it yet. We had been through so much together, and I had coaxed, encouraged and sometimes pushed them so many times over the years, but this was the *why* of why we did it together. To reach for this mountain top, and to experience it together!

We all had to conquer this mountain to apprehend what we are capable of doing in the world, not only for ourselves but for all the others depending on this planet. Grasping all the wonders of this miraculous and delicate place brings with it knowledge. We now knew that we are capable of accomplishing and contributing so much more in the world. Touching this habitat of which 98% of the world's population may never experience, adds a responsibility with accountability to share our knowledge and protect it.

We now had a new vantage point from which to appreciate how fragile this planet truly is, with first-hand comprehension that we need to take care of it and do it as a team. I felt we all heard these messages while realizing the lessons in a mediational meeting, without ever speaking a word.

In these moments, I felt grace reigning down upon my shoulders divinely imparting payment for all my toils and labors, by simply finding this place and for the landing under their wings. I would never have wandered this far from home if not for their adventurous spirits. Their youthful influence led me to know and experience such curiosities, be filled with amazement, and know with firsthand knowledge a world beyond my own backyard.

My cup is now spilling over with gratitude and adulation while vicariously living through their explorations and visions. I needed this awareness every bit as much as they did, with all the healing realms evolving through a waltz with the heavens, to push the reset button on life. Listening to the offerings in a litany of rhythms, and refocusing with harmony, enriched every cell of my being.

We sat with these lessons in silence for what seemed like hours, with my thoughts wandering back and forth like, *what are these girls thinking? Where do we go from here?* And, *how will all this play out, now and in the future?* We still have our toughest hike and day ahead, and I held each one of them in my thoughts and prayers for continued strength, growth, and awareness as we continued on the journey of unforeseen surprises.

*

Sleeping in a tent at the summit is a challenge any time of the year at the near freezing temperatures with the dampness rolling in on the low-lying clouds. We all managed to get some sleep, but I don't think anyone really had a great night of slumber. The biting cold kept us all aware or at the very least conscious of the fact that we were in the wilderness exposed to the elements. We were never in real danger staying within the confines of our shelters; however, we were painfully aware that we would not have survived outside of our tents, or without our sleeping bags at this elevation.

Chelsea passed me on the way to the outhouse-style bathroom, and we exchanged good morning pleasantries. It appeared she and I were initiating a line for the popular pit-stop first thing in the morning. While waiting patiently for our turn, I inquired, "Did you sleep well?"

She was shivering with her arms wrapped completely around herself, "Sort of, but it was sooooo cold, I kept waking up."

Commiserating with her sentiment, I confirmed the same reply, "I know what you mean; it kept me awake off and on past midnight as well."

We continued with small talk by the occupied latrine, when she announced, "Kelcy started her period last night."

"Oh no! Well, I'm sure that made her happy," I replied, half-jokingly.

"I don't think so," she replied seriously, and I knew she didn't catch my dry humor.

However, we both smiled remembering her angst and worry about having to deal with this scenario while backpacking, which had conjured up the dreaded question at our planning meeting. So my silent question was, why did it have to be her? However, all I could think of to answer myself at this moment was the expression, "what we resist, persists!" How poignant this was now. And perhaps now she'll get this lesson done early in life, and won't have to revisit it!

I didn't want to make a big deal about the news with Kelcy; however, I did want to support her with encouragement for being such a trooper. When she climbed out of her tent, I decided to catch a pulse of her demeanor, and lightly joked, "So, I hear you got your friend last night?"

Without an ounce of expression or emotion, she simply replied, "Yeah, so nice." We both attempted a half-hearted smile as a gesture, and as I turned to walk away she added, "Soooo yeah, this is the last time I name a hike, 'going with the flow!'" We both burst into laughter at this plight and moved on in silence never speaking another word of it. She really was a trooper about it all, getting on with her morning chores.

The sunrise exhibition was astounding and breathtaking, summoning all the colors from the night before but on steroids. The dome lit up in hues of scarlet, while glints of sunshine tunneled through crevices in the fluffy reddish orange clouds, depicting Jacob's Ladder all the way to earth. The sun danced its rays of light in and out of crimson for about an hour, before delivering warmth and optimism with deep blue skies.

We enjoyed a quiet breakfast watching the colorful medley of showcases pirouetting in the skies while the carpet of fluffy clouds covering the tranquil valley rolled out slowly to reveal her stark beauty. The park rangers checked in with us after breakfast for a quick briefing before starting the service projects. The girls were pretty groggy when the meeting began and seemed to be glazing over most of the opening information. However, they got up to speed once the Q&A segment started.

They were sincerely curious about the precious eco-system in the park, and were primed and ready for acquiring as much knowledge as possible, awakening with their own questions. After the consultation, we set up the photo ops and completed the session quickly. They were ready to leave for the second project when Dakota rolled out of her tent extremely sick.

It was apparent she had not been putting sunscreen on at our regular one-mile check-in stops. Her face, chest, and shoulders were covered in water blisters with her eyes and mouth swelling at an alarming rate. She was also experiencing other symptoms that we finally attributed to dehydration.

After much ado and discussion getting ready for the service project, the girls finally confessed they were all out of water. "How could this be?" I questioned because we brought enough to take us all the way through the hike. It came out that on the trip down sliding sands the morning before, Dakota had been pouring out bottles of water on our breaks to lighten up her pack. Then she started borrowing and drinking their bottles after reaching the first cabin. They were all too happy to get rid of the weight, not worrying about the latter implications. Then, drinking up all the final supplies throughout the evening and night.

The girls were now looking at one another sideways, rolling eyes and shrugging shoulders as if to say, *now what'll we do*? I certainly wasn't a happy camper to receive this bit of information; however, it wasn't the end of the world. There was one water well in the park, and it happened to be at our location. However, it wasn't potable water and certainly didn't have any of the vital nutrients needed for hiking such as we were doing at the moment.

In my first aid kit, I brought tablets for treating the water in an emergency, even though it isn't recommended to use as a main source of water, and especially for hiking. Well, this was an emergency, and we had to choke it down, literally as well as figuratively. The water had a bit of a bite to it, tasting particularly foul. We were now down to six bottles of water from mine and my husband's packs, without a choice but to treat and drink the defective water, to sustain us for the duration of the trek.

The girls discussed the possibility of scrapping the service project and heading straight to the car where we had a stockpile of water in the trunk for the last ascent. I smiled thinking, *nice try*, but didn't dare say it out loud. Today was about solutions, without pushing anybody's buttons. We had to band together now, more than ever, with no quarreling or colliding for any reason. The eco-system wasn't the only thing in a delicate balance on this day at the summit.

I suggested a solution of rationing out the six bottles of liquid we had left between the twenty-four we had to create, in hopes of diluting the taste and a few minerals amongst the eight of us. This would be a stretch depending on the heat, timing and how the day flowed, actually needing more like four bottles per person for a safe cushion. However, this would give us a bare minimum of three bottles a person, allowing us to complete the three-mile hike and service project, on top of the nearly four-mile peripheral climb straight up and out of the crater packing out all our gear.

Nobody was extremely excited about this idea, but we finally ratified it with a pact to stay the course and finish strong. Yes, we had our day cut out for us, adding another challenge to our list of capers with one more escapade, but they seemed more upbeat and ready to meet the challenge once we talked it out.

They eagerly marched away from camp in a single file line, like soldiers going off to war. I noticed their every movement with pride and admiration. They were my heroes, rallying to the occasion. It was a mile and a half each way to the work site where their project was pulling intrusive weeds away from endangered plants. They worked for hours in the hot sun on a desert terrain with cheerful hearts and enthusiasm without a single complaint. Sore and tired by noon they trekked back to camp for a late lunch and packed up our gear.

No one got terribly excited about the peanut butter and jelly sandwiches; however, they were grateful for the rest and much-needed nutrition. We still had the hardest segment ahead of our two-day outdoor survival badge to complete, with the climb straight up on switchback trails which could present new issues as their energy levels would be dropping rapidly. The backpacks were a few pounds lighter, but not so much our patience and dispositions, and I noticed the girls hitting a wall again.

I knew it was going to be an uphill challenge the whole way, so I decided to make a game out of it by making an announcement after lunch. "The first one to the top is the first one in the shower when we get home." With one bathroom at home and two days in the wilderness sweating, working and hiking, this seemed like enough of an incentive to propel them up the slopes, much less owning the bragging rights!

They were all avid sportswomen, and their competitive natures kicked in. Chelsea was the first to bite again, jumping to her feet and pulling on her gear proclaiming, "Game on!" She was ready to leave pronto, with the others scrambling to keep up.

I truly loved watching Chelsea blossom and grow over the years into a confident, capable young woman, and now she was the one usually leading the pack, challenging the others in a race to the top of the mountain. Bitter sweetness sank in as I struggled to keep from getting all melancholy, watching their antics to the finish line on this, our last expedition.

The girls now had all the incentive and propulsion they needed to make the final ascent up the steep inclines. We had done our homework, not only for this trip but over the years preparing for these moments. They were more than capable and ready for this achievement, they just didn't know it yet, until they put forth their personal bests.

Taking one look at Dakota, who was sick and ailing, seemed to be redeeming me for all my prior nagging reminders, preachy homework advice, and annoying moments. They visibly understood why I had been so steadfast in the preparation and execution of this trip, and they knew firsthand that I wasn't exaggerating any of the possible dangers. Yes, she was all part of our lessons demonstrating how not to do this hike and survive it, in a speed course of, "Do your homework 101."

Their behaviors and attitudes had taken a dramatic shift inside of only one day. Especially towards me when I geared up with the sunscreen bottle in my pesky routine of walking around putting lotion on everyone's hands to be certain they applied new coverage every single hour of the day. Heather was the only one vocal while the others objected with body language to my predictable schedule. She held the troop spokeswoman position to the very end, even soliciting her dad to get me to stop.

He would simply laugh replying, "Heather, have you met your mother, just put your hand out and get it over with and done," as he was the constant referee between her and me at this age.

I just had to let it all roll off my back, from the constant laments of my daughter saying, "We're not babies ya know," to the eye rolling glares and gestures from the rest of the pack, muttering all the while to myself, *Of course, they won't thank me now, but when they are my age they will,* silently wishing someone would have done this for me at their age so I wouldn't be spending half my time and money at a dermatologist's office.

Even now Dakota was submissively holding out a hand and accepting the emulsion, of which she had declined the entire day before. She was considered an adult on this trip and was clearly given her own choices. When it came to safety issues, I did not allow the younger girls any choice and took all the leeway of dictating responsibility. However, we could all tell at this juncture, the girls markedly had stark variances in experiences, despite the three or four years of age contrast.

Yes, this lost angel who came to our rescue was somehow vindicating me with an unspoken glance, no longer with resistance while making my rounds with a simple bottle of liquid prevention. However, being vindicated was the least of my worries. Getting this young angel with two broken wings safely off this mountain was at the forefront of my worries list, and how to get it done.

I definitely felt sorry for her, taking on such a huge lesson without proper and adequate foundations. She had been laying in a tent all day sick and weak from the effects of dehydration, coupled with the additional symptoms of second and third-degree burns. She didn't want to eat, of which was also a concern. I knew she needed some nourishment to make it up the climb: however, she was having intestinal issues that could present additional problems.

It was all still her call, and we had to go with it, and literally get her going. The girls were on the trail now, racing their way up the mountain for shower privileges and bragging rights, and we had to coax Dakota into making a vertical move. She managed the first mile fairly well, even carrying her own pack.

However, the next three miles were a test of wills, more so on my part even perhaps than hers. By the second mile, my husband and I had divided up her gear, adding it to our over burgeoning packs. By the third mile, we ran out of tissues, paper towels, and napkins, rendering Dakota's only choices for blowing her nose onto her sleeves while stopping nearly every ten steps to wail, "How much further is it?"

My husband, at this point, giving me that look again with every proliferating prod and step. We encouraged, manipulated and cajoled her every painstaking step until the last mile where we literally began pulling this weary un-winged angel with her big heart, up the narrow passageways and steep inclines. My husband took the front towing her by one arm, with me heaving from behind. On each bend or rise, I prayed more for my sake than hers, trying to locate patience, with every impetus lurch.

The looks from my husband said it all, as he communicated the unspoken language formulated through decades of marriage, and again I wisely decided to ignore him. I did not want to know what he was thinking. I was dealing with my own array of emotions, climbing out of the belly of this mountain, practically carrying another person. There was no turning back now, and the only way out was up!

Categorically to date, without a single doubt, this was the most tedious process I have ever persevered for any hike, anywhere, at any time, in any situation, whereby thrusting every one of my senses into challenge mode, irrefutably testing my mental strength, as well as my physical endurance, with an array of hallucinations, teetering somewhere between tears and laughter.

Somewhere between the bewitching eleventh hour and the parking lot, my emotions were getting so punchy that my husband wisely waved me on with amnesty in order to finish without a clash. Immediately upon surfacing to the asphalt of the parking lot, all the bane delusions abruptly drained from my being. The mere sight of this destination gave way with an exhilarating finish.

The girls were scattered around the car lounging on backpacks like pillows and began waving and cheering to acknowledge my arrival. However, the only one who jumped up to greet me was Chelsea, quickly charging my way with her bragging rights fully in tow. Waving her arms to exclaim with excitement, like Rocky doing air pushups declaring her prize, "I was the first one to the top Miss Pat, I get the shower."

We rambled to the car side by side while I fine-tuned my wits. "Good job, Chels! I kinda thought you might be the frontrunner. I had my money on you." She smiled with pride helping me remove the gear off my back. The other girls began rustling to their feet, eager to open up the car and get started with the tailgate party with goodies and rations from the trunk.

My husband and Dakota surfaced five minutes later, and the girls began cheering her all the way to the car. This parking lot celebration was in full swing passing out water and snack, with congratulations making their rounds. I was coming back to my senses, regaining a fair amount of composure, and began the usual inquiries after a long enduring hike., "So how long did it take you guys to get up here, and did you have a long wait for us to arrive?"

Chelsea couldn't wait to announce her record-breaking time, "I did it in two hours and forty-five minutes," beaming from ear-to-ear. Heather was the next to stake a claim for second place, "I was right behind her, like about five minutes." Kelcy claimed third place, and Danica and Erin strolled in several minutes behind them.

We were all laughing while having a moment on top of a mountain, simply standing around the cars, bonding and commiserating about all of the challenges. This magic could have only occurred by materializing such a feat. Their triumphs continued to morph, coming from within the laughter and discussions, as each comment materialized what had just taken place, and what was created by not giving up!

Erin was still pinching herself exclaiming, "We did it, Miss Pat," beaming with self-esteem. Sounding much like Chelsea from nine years earlier proclaiming her victory after conquering her fears of public speaking.

"Yes we did," I repeated with distinction and respect, "we absolutely did. We rocked it, and you guys rock, you guys are absolutely amazing!"

Proud couldn't even begin to cover the feelings I had for them. Just watching them bust down their walls and move through their fears elated me, just as much as it did them. Seeing them on this mountain high was worth every painstaking second to bring this moment to fruition. This is why we climb mountains, and why we have to preserve them, so we never lose our mountain top experiences!

We were all grungy, sore, tired, and ecstatic, standing on top of the world, and this was the way to finish it strong! Always in the mood for interjecting humor where adversity lingers, I realized we couldn't have humor without the resistance of struggling. Balancing it all out truly seemed the point of life to find the fun in every moment. So, I had the impulse of throwing out a great question at just the right moment. It would also give me a pulse on how quickly they were recovering, and I poked the bear once more asking, "So, who wants to do it again?"

Of course, Heather and Chelsea were chomping at the bit, "Yes!

I wanna go again! Me, me!" Erin was all smiles and nodding with them in agreement.

Kelcy rolled her eyes retorting, "Well, not right now!"

Danica chimed in putting a fine point on it, "Can we wait a week, I think I might be ready then?"

We had all but forgotten about Dakota who was still sprawled out on the grass near the car in recovery, until she raised one arm waving, eyes still closed and yelped, "I will pass!"

She brought down the house with her unmistakable punchline, and the timely rush of adrenalin transformed her off the ground and onto her feet. We began the process of getting everything packed into cars for the scramble towards home. I couldn't wait to get in line for the shower, and could already feel the warmth rushing over my head and running down my back, extinguishing the biting chill settling in my bones from the approaching setting sun and dropping temperatures.

Before loading everyone into the cars, I made one more announcement, "Oh, I forgot to tell you guys, there's one minor detail I forgot to mention about the shower," everyone looked up in attention, like *what did you say, Willis?*

They presumed I was pulling rank and was about to jump the line for the shower, with the strongest objections coming from Chelsea. I waved them back in a hand motion, laughing before it became a full-on mutiny again. "I'm jus' sayin', I forgot to tell you, if you started your period on the hike, you get to move to the front of the line for the shower, just something I forgot to mention earlier, a little tidbit of information, it's the disclaimer in the fine print."

Winking at Kelcy, who knew where I was going with this, and my way of saying, way to go girl, you were a real trooper out there! She was placing her pack in the truck chuckling in a low humming voice, "Sweeeeeet, nowww were talkin'!"

Chelsea conceded quickly, knowing she still had her bragging rights intact, which would stand the test of time. "Okay Kelcy, you can have the shower first, but then I'm next."

"Yes, you are next Chelsea, and way to go for leading the pack!" I patted her on the back for being such a good sport about it. Then beginning to get a bit sentimental again, I raised a bottle of water to all of them, "I am so proud of all of you girls. I can't even begin to tell you how much I love you guys. You guys are the bomb, now let's go home!"

Raising their bottles back and cheering, "Right back at ya, Miss Pat," along with the common sentiment, "and thank you for bringing us on the hike."

The drive home was still one of celebration and exhilaration coupled with relief, now having this big hurdle all the way behind us. They were back to themselves again, joking, laughing, and making fun of each other's most embarrassing moments, discussing all the highlights of the mountain top drama.

However, I was having a hard time following their conversations, lost in thoughts about a promise I had made to them about doing a spa day. At the big pow-wow meeting on Oahu the week before our hike, I promised to pay for the spa myself, if they completed the hike and service project, even if we ran out of troop funds. After booking and finalizing all the payments of the other activities on their fun list, this was exactly how things were shaping and transpiring. All we had left in their account for a spa experience was approximately $40 per girl. This wasn't going to go very far for a full body massage, manicures, and pedicures.

I had been working on a few leads where I worked at the Grand Wailea Spa. However, the Grand was nowhere near our leftover budget for a full treatment experience. This was a 4-star hotel with a world-class spa, and a full body massage, mani/pedi package started at $350 + tax and tip and went up from there. I worked at the salon, and even I couldn't afford to pay for a package there with my 20% discount.

I checked with some smaller resorts and spas around the area, and the prices only varied slightly with less than a $100 difference, which wouldn't help much either. I really needed to get creative and come up with some new solutions. Actually, I needed a miracle!

I had already spent $200 of my own money for the craft projects hoping the glamorous slippers would enhance the pedicure experience if it all came together, possibly in a direction I was casting out feelers. In the months prior to our trip, I began putting out petitions at work and amongst friends, to see if I could hire some freelance practitioners to set up a mini spa day in my home. There were several irons in the fire and yet nothing had panned out so far.

My thoughts were definitely preoccupied for most of the drive home now, especially with this hike in the rear-view mirror. I only had four days left to work on the setup, and remedy the situation for making good on my promise. I barely heard the jousting and conversations that were at an all-time high in the car. It was as if they were merely background noises with these thoughts tugging away at my core.

Drifting away with internal dialog, I pondered how this was yet another crossroads where I would merely have to wing it, going on a leap of faith. Mumbling a prayer to myself and the universe while driving the car on autopilot, I gave it all up to a higher power to fix this one, because here at the end, I had no way of fixing any of this without a miracle.

The numbers just simply weren't adding up. I might be able to get them a mani/pedi treatment at home, or a full body massage, but then I'd have to ask them to choose. I couldn't even begin this discussion until I had confirmation that we even had something to choose from.

We also had the Snuba boat cruise out to Molokini launching from the pier in Maalaea Harbor at 7:00am the next morning. Followed by three days in a row of action-packed fun starting at the crack of dawn, before our spa day had to be arranged igniting all the rewards. All of these factors weighed in heavily on my mind, wondering how I would even begin to set it all up, even if things started to pan out.

At this point the dreaded question filtered in from the back seat, "Miss Pat, where are we going to go for our spa day, since we finished our service project and hike?"

"Well, that is a very good question, Miss Danica; however, it's going to be a surprise!" Thinking quickly on my toes, I recovered, dodging that bullet for now! Then adding to my silent thoughts, *Yeah, well, it's actually going to be a surprise to me too!*

CHAPTER 12
IT'S SO MAUI

NEVER GIVING UP hope or faith that I had done all my homework with researching and putting out requests, I let it all go to the heavens again and got back into dealing with life. The unpacking, dinner, and shower routine went like clockwork, with everyone setting up bags for the boat excursion and the 5:00am scramble to Maalaea Harbor.

Again, we packed the finished bags into the trunks for a quick getaway at dawn. The troops were tuckered and tucked in quickly at the end of this long day without a single reminder for retiring. It seemed like they had traveled thousands of miles in just under three days, and with lights out early I was able to concentrate on the spa planning again.

I sat down to meditate and enlist yet another prayer when the phone rang with a call from one of my homework enlistees. It was a massage therapist who had just graduated from training, whom I found through a friend at work. She was just starting out with a home-based practice and was located only a couple blocks away from my house.

After introductions and relaying our needs, it turns out she was a Girl Scout growing up. In light of their accomplishments, recent hike, and service project, she offered to waive her usual fee of $55 an hour and take in all six girls for $25 apiece. This was a Godsend and just the break I'd been looking for. I was hoping to find more than one massage therapist because this meant it would take six hours to get everyone done. However, we had to go with what we could find and somehow make it work. Now this being our only offer in a price range I could work with, we set up a tentative plan.

She also offered me a full body massage for the same lowered rate; however, I wouldn't be able to afford the time or the money handling all the last-minute details. Spa day was scheduled on the last day, with the girls catching the last flight to Oahu at 10:30pm. We would have to deliver them to the airport by 9:30pm, which translated into leaving my home by 9:00pm.

We were locked into this tight schedule because we had to rely on my husband for help shuttling them around in two cars, and this was the only time he could lend us for vacation from work. Making everything work on this schedule was our only option if we were to have a spa day! I thanked the Almighty for coming through again and gave it all up to the universe to figure out the rest.

The next day we had a blast on the boat!! Much like our very first cookie blaster party which earned us a trip on a Catamaran in Waikiki. This trip was a floating party of food, fun in the sun, snorkeling, and site seeing along the southern coastline of Maui. On this party barge, they were truly letting down their hair and enjoying the ride with an extra appreciation for the lumber it took for securing such a reward.

I could feel them reflecting on the journey, noticing the connections within their eyes that said, *yes, we did it*, as we cruised along the shoreline viewing the mountain range from a new vantage point. The gleam and sparkle said it all, but the graceful smiles said it with a sense of pride. They were on a whole new ride, skimming along the water still on a mountain high.

Our boat tour anchored for lunch in a cozy alcove located in the middle of the harbor about six miles from the main shoreline, at an islet known as Molokini. The coral island, teeming with tropical life, was formed by an extinct volcano crater that collapsed into the ocean's floor, leaving the tip of the cone protruding from the water's surface area. The semicircle atoll produces a perfection of shallow waters in an aquarium procreation for snorkeling and viewing the local fish in their natural habitat.

We had a full view of the mountain in all her splendor for the day on the water, drinking up her beauty and relaxing from her exertions, accentuating the contrasts from the toils on the dusty trails to the lush ocean treasures of abundant resources abounding everywhere. We were connecting more than just our local cornucopia of geological possessions. This new vantage point was beginning to take flight in their mind's eye, without even realizing they were assembling such decisions. Ideas about their world, their futures and their dreams formulating with the connections.

During the mooring party, the boat's captain introduced himself and inquired about the girls he noticed posing at the bow of the ship for a group photo. He picked up on something unique with their party and asked if they were celebrating a special event. We had a discussion about their accomplishments and tenure together, as well as the revelry taking place on his tour. He was very impressed with their achievements, sharing that he had lived on Maui over forty years and had visited the summit dozens of times; however, he confessed he would never have attempted anything as brave as a couple of miles up there, much less carrying thirty pounds of weight doing it.

He asked me to write down a brief bio about the girls and the troop with their accomplishments, along with their most recent exploit on the mountain. He wanted to honor them by making an announcement during the voyage back to the dock. During his announcement, he asked all the girls to come up to the bridge, so he could personally meet them and shake their hands.

After a lively greeting, he announced that each one of the girls could sit at the helm and steer the boat (with his apprentice of course) conveying, "If you can carry a thirty-pound backpack sixteen miles at 10,000 feet on that mountain, and survive for two days working in the hot sun, then you can certainly drive a boat."

Tipping his hat towards them, he smiled, "And my hats off to you ladies. Who's driving the boat first?"

Of course, it would be Chelsea stepping up to the plate first; she'll never have to be convinced again of the apropos of being assertive and taking a risk. She also found the perfect opportunity to remind the captain she was the first one on our ascent to climb the last four miles out of the crater. "Then you have earned the wheel first young lady," and he proudly showed her the complexities of the stern.

True to form, Heather grabbed the power of the rudder next like she was hanging on for dear life. She was the most petite one of the group, barely coming up to my shoulders. It took all the strength in her stiff arms with a white-knuckle grip to steer the massive wheel of this fifty-foot catamaran. With her hair completely vertical peeling backward from the wind, she glanced over her right shoulder spying a peak at the mountain, back towards me winking, and back to wearing the captain's shoes, like she knew exactly what she was doing.

They were stretching their wings that day sailing across the sea, each one at the helm of a vessel appropriately called *Her Majesty*. I embraced these coming of age moments in admiration of their abilities, grace, and beauty. I triumphed within these conquests, watching with awe when they arose face-to-face with their own greatness. *Does it get any better than this in life?* I wondered, witnessing this story unfold with its trials, trails, and treks all the way around the track, to finish with a full course of grandeur.

After a full day of rewards, reflections, relaxation, and rejuvenation on the boat, we were more than ready to find our land legs again.

We scrambled for home with the lineup and shower routine, where I was pleasantly pleased to hear them negotiate a schedule without my assistance. They were becoming more like siblings now, only better, without all the rivalry bloodlines usually insist on consuming. I still had the spa agenda poking for my attention, and wanted to urgently answer a phone message from a co-worker who was responding about the manicures and pedicures.

After unpacking the cars and setting everyone up with dinner, I called my good friend Cheryl to discover she had recruited another friend from work to take on our project. They would both come to my home, set up all the necessities, and commit their services for the remaining amount left in the coffers of $15 per girl for both the manicure and pedicure.

This was another Godsend, and unheard of, considering they usually received five times that amount going out on location for their amenities. They would also be donating their trades to this project by granting the waiver in price. This was the shot in the dark I was looking for, and more like a miracle appearing out of nowhere presenting itself as a gift. Cheryl also let me know the other friend, Laurie, was a former Girl Scout and was proud to be contributing towards this reward for their years of diligence, service, and hard work.

I sat in contemplation, *so this is how it works, floating down the raging river of life. If we take care of all the right things for today, check all the gear, follow through, stay together and strong, we will reach our destination with everything we need and more. These lessons were all coming full circle now, not just for the girls but for me as well.*

It's all about girls helping girls, women showing girls, then girls teaching women never to give up, and sometimes it takes the child to raise up the village. They are the ones that showed me how to stay the course, trust and have faith, and how to give back. They showed me what this life and the journey are all about. How pivotal and poignant that the leader becomes the pupil.

*

We still had three more days of fun, filled with exhilaration, while we worked out the bathroom and sunrise routine, which were finally down to a science. It was time to head back up the mountain for thrills, chills, and daredevil stunts, careening over canyons and valleys on zip-lines. This time, we would be zig-zagging our way down the mountain slopes, screaming with excitement completing the ascent on the fast track, aerial style. The tour was also an ecoenvironmental guided hiking tour with a fair amount of hiking in between each extravagant trust fall.

At one point on the tour, one of the guests in another party began complaining about how much walking we had to do, compared to how much flying there was on the zip-lines. In total, we actually only walked one and a half miles for the entire trek, with about eight zip-lines breaking up the hike. Erin caught my eye with a smile, and I winked back signaling that we both remembered our little conversation of a few days earlier. She nuzzled up, walking closely to whisper, "Should I tell them about going with the flow?"

We both snickered, and I replied, "Probably not a good plan on this hike, but *it is* all perspective." She agreed with a wide-eyed expression while nodding, and we plodded along in silent appreciation under the shaded trees of the lush green forests, occasionally catching a spectacular view along the stroll. We were now canvassing the four and five thousand foot levels of this mammoth mountain, taking in all the splendor and entertainment she had to offer.

After the colossal feats of the morning, we traveled the upcountry back roads to the Ulapalakua Ranch General Store for a barbecue lunch. The old countryside settings of the Paniolo (meaning cowboy) town is located across from the Maui Winery, which still holds irreplaceable qualities of the horse and buggy era.

The views include more than half the island's south shoreline, all the way to three of the surrounding islands at this 1,800-foot level. This landscape still donning remnants of the delicate purple jacaranda tree blossoms for which Maui is famous for. The towering eucalyptus, canopied banyan trees and tautness of Norfolk pines openhandedly enthralls nature's handy work painting its own canvas, also known in many famous renderings from local artists.

We bonded over a hearty fare in this picturesque setting of karmic delight, later exploring the grounds of a rich and historical past through century-old structures, posing for photos in the circle of cypress trees planted by King Kalakaua commemorating the dance for royalty and merchant sailors, and the cannon which would sound for the king's arrival. We finished in front of the oldest stately tree on the grounds, and perhaps in the islands, once used to make ship masts due to its perfect growth, strength, and durability.

We added two more stops with tours at the Lavender Farm and Surfing Goat Cheese Farm on the way back to our home-based coastline retreat, learning about commerce in local businesses. With another full slate of experiences under our belts, let's just say, we called this day a wrap with success, and there were no arguments or hesitations about turning in early. Lights out early for the girls meant I could make final preparations for a spa day with one more phone call, wrapping up my day as well.

One more friend left a message about a resort just a mile from my home that was having a membership drive and special for local residents to join their pool spa club facilities. I had been a guest at the pool with my friend the month before, which had Terme hydrotherapy tubs overlooking the ocean. It was a relaxing experience for sure with whirlpools, plunge pools, cascading waterfall massage fountains, sauna, and steam rooms included with the membership.

The first-time annual fee was $200 with a sponsor. She thought we might be interested using this for our spa day and offered to sponsor me for the discount. My family could use the pool all year after joining, but I explained that we had used all of the budget already. My personal budget was full as well with all the crafts, extra expenses and contingencies adding up.

The only place I might have been able to borrow funds would have been Heather's money in the troop account for her travel back to Oahu. This money was left in the troop funds for Heather matching the cost of a roundtrip ticket since she did not use troop funds to travel to Maui. The funds were earmarked for traveling to Oahu when she wanted to staff a PCCS camp in the future.

I could use this money now and have her travel money available within a few weeks, replacing it well before PCCS camp rolled around. However, I told her I needed to sleep on it, for getting a feel of how things might flow altogether with the spa day plans. Sleep on it I did, and now my cup ran over with ideas, wondering if I should add on the pools.

After rest, careful thought, and a big breakfast, I put together some scenarios of how it could all work. With my home centered within a mile of the pools on one side and the massage therapist on the other, we could fit everything in by shuttling everyone on the hour. I decided to seize the moment and go with the membership, now really able to close this chapter of the spa planning and get on with the last two days of fun.

After riding hard and putting everyone up wet all week, the second to the last day would be about resting, relaxing and more low key for sure. For starters, we all slept in for a change and enjoyed breakfast on the patio in daylight. Then we meandered out to Big Beach, known for its long, pristine white sandy shores and formidable short curling waves famous for boogie boarding. If the interest and energy held up after the beach, we'd add a shopping spree in the late afternoon and/or evening.

The leisurely start and fifteen-minute drive from our home were just what I needed, besides resting in a beach chair by the ocean for half the day. I decided to start writing a poem that described my experiences with the girls and the troop while reflecting with the lull of the tides.

We planned to have a pizza dinner picnic on the beach, just at the end of my street for our last night together. At the conclusion of our spa day would be the perfect time for a sunset closing with the badges, pins, and accolades they had earned on this trip and throughout the year. We could complete everything by 9:00pm before making the trek for the airport.

Everything was coming together as it should, including the timing and all the resources, as if I had planned it that way all along, knowing full well I winged it every step of the way!

Most importantly I would be giving them a Ten-Year pin, which apparently doesn't occur very often for Girl Scouts. When I tried purchasing the pins at the council store on Oahu, they informed me they were not a stocked item and would have to be special ordered. I inquired as to why this was the case, as they had so many hundreds of other items in stock.

The clerk simply replied, "Because we don't get requests for them very often." This rather surprised me while she further dumbfounded me by adding, "and I don't think I've put in more than a half a dozen orders in the past five years that I've worked here."

We talked a bit more about the reasons why this might be the case while she put together my order. We further discussed some of the possibilities which might be contributing to the sudden dropoff rate after 3-6 years, and I walked away feeling lucky, special and honored to have had all our remarkable years.

I wasn't so sure I would be able to express adequately all my thoughts and feelings at such an extraordinarily unique occurrence for our sunset closing ceremony. Especially in lieu of the pending airport travels shortly thereafter. Expressing my feelings in person was not exactly one of my fortes, however, putting them down on paper was one of my greatest strengths. I decided to go with my strengths here, considering I really didn't want to screw this one up.

I began noting all the things that stood out and what I appreciated the most. Completing the list on the beach made it easy to continue scribbling lines after we changed venues to Queen Kaahumanu Mall for the shopping spree that evening. The way I had it figured, we would be there for a while, so I perched on a bench in the center of the mall, with my notepad, hot tea, and a good book.

The girls took off in a posse and knew exactly where to find me at the end of their shopping escapades. I was a happy camper settled in to get some work done and otherwise get some serious rest. Within forty-five minutes they were all back and ready to go home! "Well, that didn't take long," I mentioned packing up my belongings to leave.

"It doesn't take me long to spend the money my dad gave me," Kelcy lamented while rolling her eyes at the rest of the girls. They all nodded in concurrence, and we were suddenly all done with the shopping!

Now I thought and smiled to myself on the way to the car, *Wow, this has gotta be some kind of world record for getting teens with time and money to exodus a mall, perhaps I have found the cure for consumerism, and I can figure out a way to market this concept.*

Yes, they appeared to be tuckered out, and after the full week of exploits, shopping must not have had the same appeal. Perhaps Mother Nature herself is the antidote, and she holds all the answers to alleviate materialism. Leaving that thought for another day, I was relieved to get home early for a barbecue dinner on the porch, fashioned much in the same way we had ushered in the week, relaxing and socializing about all the fun we had in common, shared Hawaiian style with tiki torches a blazing.

Reward day was up next at the top of the schedule for a grand finale finish in comforting proportions. Early to rise the next morning, I packed up a continental breakfast, and we started spa day by the poolside overlooking the ocean with warm muffins, fruit, yogurt, snacks, and drinks. Dakota attended all of our excursions for the week, and this was no exception, she most certainly had earned this reward as well.

The girls decided amongst themselves who would go first, and the others stayed by the pool with Dakota's aunt Laurie, while I chauffeured them in rotation to their appointments. My friends let themselves into the condo, setting up for nail treatments while we enjoyed a quiet morning relaxing in the sun.

After soaking up the sun during breakfast, the first three started in the soaking tubs and massage pools for a warm up. We began the first shuttle of appointments with one girl at a massage and two girls at a time for nails. This rotation commenced hourly until everyone had a treatment. The first group completed went back to the pool for relaxation in the sun or had the option of taking a nap in my air conditioned bedroom, already set up with soft music or movies.

During my wait between shuttles, I began handwriting all my reflections and thoughts about our ten years of passage together onto notecards, to go along with their handcrafted slippers and scrapbooks. This, of course, was a part of me to take home in remembrance of our distinguished journey as a troop. These poems which summed up my feelings, thoughts and memories, were ready by the end of the day, sealed in envelopes for our sunset graduation on the beach.

CHAPTER 13
TAKING FLIGHT

WITH EVERYONE REFRESHED, rested and revived, and with all the bags packed into the cars for travel to the airport, we made our way to the beach for a sunset picnic dinner. Takeout pizza was the tall order on the menu, and we covered all the favorites, adding large homemade baked cookies for dessert.

Sporting their personally designed glimmering slippers, we located our blankets on a grassy spot instead of the sand, for keeping everyone's perfectly manicured feet clean and ready for a flight, perched just high enough on a ridge to see the tumbling waves against the backdrop of the setting sun. On a perfect night, for a perfect ending, to a perfect week, the solar glow was basking on the mountain's mystique as if to highlight all her majesty's best features.

We experienced Mother Nature's paint brush swirling in her scarlet shades of passion, burning against the contrast of the sun dipping into the ocean. Soaking up the *aina* (Hawaiian for 'gifts of the land') and drinking in the beauty all abounding, ushered in a sense of divine serenity suited for this prestigious evening of dining by the sea.

After connecting with the earth and filling our souls with nourishment, we got underway with an informal meeting rich within our tradition of sharing in a circle. Seated on blankets Indian style, reminiscent of our original meetings with yet another déjà vu moment, we delved back in time regarding all the miles we had indeed traveled together. Yielding to the present, we each took turns sharing about the important lessons we had learned on this trip.

Of course, Chelsea would go first; it was now her pertinent right and duty, and we were definitely all smiles watching her doing so with confidence. "The best thing I liked about this week was climbing that mountain, (pointing up to it) and what I learned most is that I am stronger than I thought I was, and I can do a lot more than I thought I could."

Kelcy surprised us next, jumping in quickly, "What I liked the most about this week was climbing that mountain, (as she glanced up at it) and what I learned the most was I actually do like backpacking and hiking and earning a survival badge." We all roared with laughter as she threw in the punch line, "Oh yeah, and I won't die from starting my period while I'm doing it," pitching up the hilarity to new levels of screams and squeals.

Danica spoke up next, observing that Kelcy's punch line was a tough act to follow, and she too chose the mountain as her favorite segment of the week. Erin and Heather also confirmed their choices, making it unanimous. After every single encounter of the week, they were all on the same page; the overnight backpacking hike was the highlight!

Who would have thought? The thing they feared the most. The biggest hurdle of the week that took the most effort to bust through, with grit, blood, sweat, and tears, versus the most pleasurable or thrill-seeking, was the one they would choose. This was the all-time favorite, despite all the other fun and cool stuff we did, including the spa treatments, which did get an honorable mention, this was the top contender.

After giving voice to their affirmations, and paramount to our lesson, we sat in silence allowing time to for these words to truly sink in with the significance they had or will have on our lives from this day forward. Touching on the core beliefs in these validating moments was one of constructing a legacy from within. The seeds sewn many years ago revealed basic truths about themselves that were now taking root within these accomplishments, not only from the past week but also throughout the past decade as well.

Sitting in a contented orb, exploring and connecting through our thoughts of mutual understanding, brought these lessons home not only for the girls but for me as well. I was still connecting all the dots about the whining, crying, and fear they had prior to the hike and how it needed to be addressed. More importantly, how it *wanted* to be addressed. They would never have been happy with themselves taking the easy way out. It simply would have prolonged the inevitable maturing process if I had coddled them and allowed them to give in to their fears rather than bust through them.

These moments were another summit experience of reconnecting everything from our relationship and connection to the mountain while beholding one another in esteem and simply confirming all our knowledge through a smile or a nod. Yes, our mountain top experience ended as a pinnacle on the beach, and would forever be our link. It was now tattooed on our hearts, stored within our cells, and would stay a part of our being, conveyed and unspoken in this unbroken circle.

I knew what these girls were made of, and I always saw their greatness; however, I didn't see any of this coming a week prior, much less ten years ago. They simply and absolutely astounded me, at their tender ages. Without question, I could feel their state of contentment and serenity, accompanied by joy, of which took me years of research to find and land upon. It seemed we were viewing life now from nearly the same vantage point, magically transformed from little girls, into capable young women within a span of less than a week. We were all getting things into perspective now, with knowing what is truly important in life and what isn't even worth mentioning.

Every chamber and ventricle of my heart were bursting at the seams with gratification, just from all the knowing. From knowing these incredible young ladies and sharing in all their gifts. From knowing their story, their journey, and every hurdle, challenge and battle they had to overcome. For knowing the strides they have most certainly made. And for knowing, I made the right choices when I was called to serve some ten years earlier. Now knowing this was a rare opportunity that only comes along once in a lifetime, and I had the wherewithal to seize it, not letting it elude me.

Yes, knowing was my apex in all of this, and knowing that this awareness was and is a gift, perhaps one of the greatest gifts in life. To know that I know, and not second guess myself, was and is an amazing feeling, much like standing on a mountaintop in the euphoric high, witnessing all the heavens swirling in beneath my feet with a confirmation that there is more to life than just breathing, eating and taking up space. Discovering, knowing, and connecting all of this is the point of life. The fact that we know and connect with other individuals, other species, other places for the greater good of all in its entirety is what sets us apart as a species. Using collaboration for creation of amazing feats, act of courage, selflessness, and bravery is the real point in life. This knowledge and growth which all came from within, was most certainly attained through new experiences, revealing strengths I didn't even know I had.

While exposing these power points of existence through experiential lessons, another revelation occurred. The only way I was able to attain this knowledge was by stopping all the chatter, internal noise and external distractions, interruptions, and madness, and by simply listening to what was truly important, coming from within. Then, by taking action with and from these messages of which I heard, and inherently already knew, I affirmed for myself that life really does have meaning and purpose. Divulging these lessons about life gave new meaning to my purpose.

Coming full circle with these irresistible toothless Brownies, turned competent capable Cadettes, and uncovering my capacity to do more, give more, and ultimately receive more than I gave, in a full karma exchange of love, life, learning and purpose, I truly understood Horace's famous quote from his Odes, in which he wrote, "carpe diem, quam minimum credula postero," which has been translated in many ways such as, to pick or pluck and enjoy, seize, or make use of the day, or pluck the day, as it is ripe and simply shortened to, enjoy the moment or seize the day.

Upon further reflection in these few moments, I truly felt like I understood his meaning which translates into "seize the day, but put very little trust in tomorrow," as the future is unforeseen! Powerful words written centuries ago by a Roman poet, yet more apropos than ever, and befitting for this day. He isn't trying to say you should ignore the future, but rather do all you can today to make your future better and trust that everything you do in the moment will fall into place for the future by taking this action now and in today. I truly understand these words more now than ever, watching them play out over a decade in this dance of life.

Life is poetic, prophetic and all-encompassing with a point and purpose to everything. These young ladies had and have truly given my life purpose with new meanings. Without a doubt, the exchange turned into a beautiful waltz of wisdom and learning about life together.

*

In keeping with all our traditions and the urgency of the ever ticking clock, I rummaged for my famous box, housing the precious accolades for which we honored their achievements. They were mused with an unusual amount of zest and vigor that I'd never witnessed before. I was delighted to experience their refreshing new demeanors ushered in and parceled mostly by success. I handed each award around the circle, pointing out the qualities and attributes we learned and followed for earning each such distinction.

This was, by and large, the least ceremonious and informal bridging party we had ever held, yet it felt the most important and sincere. It was no longer some rote gesture moving them on to fun stuff of the past. This was now the main event of which they were now fully vested by earning and attaining these priceless merits and metals. The look of self-worth was sprawled across the smiles amidst each deserving accolade I bestowed. I knew they were still standing tall on a mountain top, at the top of the world, while sitting on a blanket right in front of me, on a beach. I knew instinctively they owned this prized distinction and would wear it wherever they went. It was obtained, secured, and achieved because they faced off and conquered some of their greatest fears.

They were my heroes breaking down these walls, kicking through the barriers, and moving mountains to find their victories. I knew at this very moment we had created something special that would surpass the test of time. I knew now they could begin flying solo, equipped with all their certainty and convictions tucked away in their new tool boxes, covered with an arsenal of confidence for keeping them safe, aiding in their growth, and lifting them to new heights for playing a bigger game in life. I knew this was the moment for passing the baton and empowering the next generation to transmit their ripples out into the world.

In all the decorations they received on this day, the least of these were measured in a tangible sense. However, they earned for the year, seven badges from experiences with hiking, eco-environmental, backpacking, overnight survival, aquatic, business commerce, and travel, a tenth one year pin, a tenth honor troop charm, a tenth aloha ambassador rocker, two PCCS Camp patches, a Leadership pin, a Senior Bridging patch, and a Ten-Year service pin. These tributes and honors would complete their Cadette sashes, bridging them up to Senior Scouts for another three years, if they so choose to sign up again.

Without exception, they each did just that, proclaiming their desire to continue as Senior Scouts, or at the very least, stay involved by mentoring younger troops and staffing the PCCS camps at Pamualu. Heather would fly over to attend these events with them on weekends, and still had her flight waiting in the wings from the troop travel funds. With the pesky clock still ticking, I started winding down the meeting retrieving the trusty box holding the handwritten note cards with my final sentiments.

*

The girls all looked around and smiled as if they were the ones giving out the awards, and before I could pass out the envelopes addressed to each one of them, Danica pulled a padded envelope from behind her seated position. "Here Miss Pat, we have something we would like to give you first." Handing me the envelope from across the circle, they all recited in unison, "This is from all of us to you."

Looking at the bulging exterior thinking they must have written notes as well, I said, "Maybe I should read these tonight after I put you guys on the plane." All at once they shouted, "No, no, no. We want you to read it now."

I can certainly tell when I've been vetoed, so began opening up the envelope. They were unusually squirmy bursting with excitement, and being the perceptive individual that I am, I could tell this was of huge importance to them. I was also profoundly flattered that they had taken the time to make this gesture of gratitude, thinking at this timely and poignant juncture that some of my behaviors had definitely rubbed off on them. All of these thoughts burgeoning from my monkey brain while exchanging our appreciations towards one another, and how blessed I was again!

These fleeting thoughts occurred in the few seconds it took to open the envelope and find a card with six yellow Labrador puppies lined up in a row on the cover. They donned all the innocent cuddly cuteness of soft fuzzy fur, heads cocked sideways, and tongues hanging out, with the card reading, "THANKS, for giving all you give."

I was already getting emotional just looking at the words and glancing up at them I said, "Thank you, this is so awesome. How did you ever find such a perfect fit?" Then interjecting my humor as I always do, to avoid becoming too emotional, "Look, they look just like you guys when I first met you, all cuddly, bouncy and sweet, see there's Heather the runt, and Danica the tall one, and Kelcy the serious one, and…" They were getting anxious, interrupting, "Open it, Miss Pat."

"Okay, okay, okay." I opened the card to have a huge pile of twenty dollar bills fall into my lap. Still not registering what had just taken place, I scooped up the money asking, "What is this?"

As if they had rehearsed it, they all chimed in at once, "That is our shopping money!" And I was rendered speechless! For the first time in my whole life, I didn't have the words. They had me at "thank you for all you gave," on the front cover, but this went completely over my head and out of the solar system to even comprehend.

Choking back the tears that were about to burst like a dam, I tried to ask but couldn't, with the words now caught in my throat. They knew they had me flabbergasted and began to explain away, "We wanted you to have it since you showed us it was more important to take care of others and the environment than just thinking about ourselves first." And "we thought you would need it to help with the expenses you have with gas, tips, extra food and stuff you always got us over the years."

I was so overcome with emotion that I don't remember who was speaking what, I simply remember the messages and how perfectly they were conveyed. The dam was finally broken and spilling down my face, and all I could manage to utter was a squeaky, high-pitched, "Thank you." Period. That was all that was coming out. There was so much more inside fighting to reach the surface, but that was it for now, with all my senses firing, and absconding with my vocals.

I sat in my pile of emotions trying to read the messages on the inside, both printed and written by the girls. Making matters worse and invoking even more emotion, the inside read, "Thank you for being you!"

By the time I got to Kelcy's note, it was completely over; I was downright balling with each sentiment of confirmation. She was sometimes my biggest adversary, teaching me the most about my own resistance and how to dig inside looking for more answers. She put it all on the card and said it so eloquently, "Thanks for all the time you spent with us, whether I liked it or not, because I appreciated it all and the most. I'm glad you were our leader, 'cause these ten years were awesome."

I had to pause to finish, now grappling for more air. My daughter, who was always the most vocal and outwardly the most critical, rarely ever showed any signs of appreciation, signed the card, "Thanks for being a great leader, and a good mom!" This sentiment alone was moving a mountain for her at 15 years old while we were experiencing a great deal of normal teenage *mother-daughter rivalry.*

After squeaking out, another "thank you" and giving each one a hug, the contagion of emotion picked up its pace, and we were all quite a sight, sitting on a blanket in a circle, hugging and crying on a world class tourist destination without so much as a stare. I remember thinking the tourist must be wondering what is going on over in that loop? Are they thinking "Wow, we don't want to go home either, but that's a little over the top." I always found humor to bring me back to earth.

Sitting back motionless in our never-ending circle, I wondered what would come next. Humbled and overwhelmed, drying up my face, they took the reins and began speaking first. Each one pro-fessing a statement about her convictions in life, and her future. They each gestured at the mountain nodding and exclaiming "If I can climb that mountain, I can become a teacher…an actress… a designer."

One by one they each stated their goals, taking up each other's hands and sealing their convictions within the circumference of our group. The last of their declarations came to cover yet another orbit, "and when we get our goals, we'll be back to this island and that mountain to remember this day, and this week, to remember that we can accomplish anything we put our minds to."

Where was all this coming from, this wisdom beyond their years, as if every lesson we covered over a decade funneled into a vacuum and came out this vortex as a completely evolved species? Who were these girls I had been prodding, pushing and mentoring for a tenth of a century?

I was simply astonished, speechless again, and all I could do was smile, nodding with agreement. I was on their ride now, pulled up in the thrust of their wings, watching them soar with pride while gliding through the lesson as their trusted pupil.

I didn't think we could get any higher than the mountain tops on this journey, but they showed me otherwise, scooping me up under their wings and taking me on the ride of my life! This was quite the expedition, and what a party we had, doing everything together in a sisterhood of growing, loving and learning together, expanding our wings to create some of the greatest gifts in life!

We held hands smiling until time dictated the schedule, and all I could muster and say without tearing up again was, "I am so proud of you girls right now," alongside the clock keeping me on an emotional checkpoint. We had to pack up the party and make the dash for the airport. The curbside drop-off was another moment of difficult goodbyes, however, managing nearly drama-free with all the urgency to catch a plane.

*

The drive home was another moment for reflection and pulled me on the emotional roller coaster of seeing them so grown up and independent. I cried this time with joy and release filling up my heart, for all that they had shown me turning into grace. First, leading them out of duty, evolving into love, sometimes with my fears, but always with respect, and turning to the universe when all else was lost but trust.

There was a sense of sadness seeing them rush away, yet it was time to let the seeds we planted germinate and grow for the harvest that will surely flourish in their steady flight paths. I knew these moments laced in bitter sweetness were only a fleeting feature because I was forever changed by meeting these young ladies, with all their gifts bestowed.

While sitting at a stop light I heard a jet overhead thrusting into the heavens, poking my head out the window, I looked skyward with a thought, *Yes, you guys are definitely ready to take flight now, so where do we go from here? Well, up of course!*

IN SUMMARY

APPROXIMATELY THREE YEARS after our life-changing hike on Haleakala, my second oldest son asked me to escort some of his friends visiting from the mainland into the crater of the summit on a 13-mile day hike. My son was off island, and couldn't get over to Maui to take them. He didn't hesitate to ask his 50-something-year-old mom to pick them up at the airport and show them the sites, now that I was a seasoned backpacker. I was a bit honored and humbled being asked, knowing it was something that never would have happened if I hadn't 'spread my wings' with the girls some years earlier. However, after our experience with Dakota and a couple more hair-raising experiences on the mountain, I was a bit reluctant with saying "yes" right away.

I was now being more careful and discerning about who I took into this foreboding mountain wilderness! Shortly after our maiden hike, I escorted my grandson's therapist and his four adult brothers who were all Eagle Boy Scouts visiting from the mainland, and a Maui friend who was a retired motorcycle police officer from San Francisco. On this particular hike, I accidently took a bad fall and severely sprained my ankle. With the quick response from my highly experienced fellow hikers and our abundantly equipped first-aid kits, I was up and walking within 15 minutes, even though it was a bit dicey putting weight on the joint. We weren't sure if something more serious was going on, like a cracked or broken bone.

Nevertheless, we took measures for reducing the swelling, and I got moving quickly. I definitely didn't want to call or wait for rescue efforts from the park rangers, after watching this scenario play out firsthand on our maiden hike to the summit. The injured person waited all day, in throbbing pain, under the blistering sun, for the dispatch to arrive; then rode out slowly on the back of a horse, in the dark, cold, freezing rain, with temperatures below 40 degrees, on foot-trails three feet wide, at the edge of 4,000-foot cliffs without support rails. Needless to say, I said, "No thank you!"

Keeping the alternatives in the forefront of my thoughts, along with a few Tylenol, was the only thing that pushed me through the throbbing pain and thrust me up the bluffs before dark! I only had to hike another seven miles to get out of the crater safely, with nearly half the distance straight up the mountain cliffs, it was a challenge for sure. Revisiting the memories from time-to-time of dragging another injured person up the rigorous mountain terrain, while counting my blessings that it was only my weary carcass I had to push this time. It turned out nothing was broken. However, it took weeks for the swelling to go down, and months of painful rehab to completely heal.

On an additional hike with a friend who is a native of Michigan, I experienced yet another close encounter with Mother Nature letting us know who is in command of this massif topography. I wrote the story down, later winning a writing competition about how confident my friend was tackling a hike on a mountain, in the Hawaiian Islands. Well you know, because he was "from Michigan."

"How difficult can it be?" He questioned when we began discussing the possible dangers, challenges, necessary equipment, and precautions we would be taking. I could tell by his statements and nonchalant tone he wasn't going to heed my stern warnings about this unforgiving mountain at extreme altitudes, so I packed double gear just to be certain.

Our morning started off at a normal pace with perfect weather, and everything we planned to do was on schedule. Our three-day backpacking adventure began on the ever famous "Sliding Sands Trail," and without a hitch, we reached the barren desert floor of the summit depression within a few hours.

A welcome relief from misting rain blessed our walk, with the rising mercury scorching the desert like atmosphere upon reaching the flats in the bowl-shaped depression. Within an hour the light misting turned into high winds, pelting rain, and zero visibility making the weight of our packs twice as heavy, along with wind-chill factors dropping into the freezing range. Dark clouds moved in quickly, and we had a situation brewing on our hands.

Walking into the gale force winds we had to keep our bodies folded at the waist, eyes pointed to the ground, with backpacks riding vertically in order to push forward without being knocked down. By the time we reached the halfway point at the first cabin for our breaking point and lunch, we were in a full monsoon. The winds were gusting well over 60 mph, hail the size of grapes, and the cabin was locked with no one around. We quickly took shelter by putting our backs against a wall of the cabin, huddled like a tripod, standing our backpacks in front of us, while holding slickers over the top and sides to keep from being pelted to death by the ice storm.

The temperature was dropping rapidly, and luckily I had packed the extra gloves, head gear, and jackets in a waterproof stash. In these conditions, it didn't take long for these items to be rendered useless and eventually soaked along with all our gear in tow. They did, however, for the short term, keep us protected from the elements long enough for some much-needed relief in the frigid conditions, to get some rest and nourishment while hunkering down to try waiting out the storm. We later learned that the rangers closed the summit trails a few hours after we started.

After an hour of hanging on for dear life, we dashed towards the next cabin, which was our converging point to meet up with a volunteer group for the main purpose of our expedition, doing a service project. We had to make the three-and-a-half mile hike before dark when the weather and freezing temperatures could really become life threatening. We pushed through the torrid winds, heavy rain and sleet blowing sideways, in the bone-chilling conditions with backpacks doubling in weight by taking on all the elements. Just before nightfall, we collapsed on the floor of the warm cabin with hypothermia, completely drenched, frozen and depleted.

The next day we still had to climb nearly four miles up the crater in similar conditions, to get out for medical attention. Starting out with dry clothing that we hung overnight by the wood burning stove, food and rest gave us the edge to complete the hike without a rescue. However, it did not prevent us from becoming very ill at the end, and I had a severe case of bronchitis, with my friend not so lucky ending up with full blown pneumonia.

So, I was a little more than a bit hesitant to take on a trip through the summit with folks I'd never met, even for a day hike. I told my son I would only consider it after spending a little time with them to assess whether or not they were ready for such an ominous hike as this. Based on their levels of knowledge and experience for high elevation hikes, the homework they had done about this particular mountain, and the gear they packed, I determined they were ready for the excursion, and we set out for the summit the next day. Oh, and one more thing, they had to view the training video at Park Headquarters.

*

While they watched the video, I was obtaining a day permit for hiking at the front desk. One of the park rangers approached me asking,

"You look so familiar to me, do we know each other from somewhere"? I shared where I lived, and we began covering the list of our activities to see if we would have ever crossed paths. After coming up empty, I suggested perhaps we worked together when I brought up the girl troop or worked on the mountain with the 'Friends of Haleakala.'

"Nope, that wasn't it either!" We finally left it at that, and moved on to another conversation, never really figuring out why I looked so familiar because I didn't really have the same familiar connection he did. While chatting about all the changes in the park a few minutes later, my new friends were shouting from the video room, "Hey Pat, come here! Isn't that you? There on the video? That's you isn't it?"

"Well, yes it is!" I laughed, mumbling to myself, "We did make the video after all."

"Look, you are wearing the same khaki shirt and camouflage pants," they were pointing towards the screen. Sure enough, I was still dawned in my favorite comfortable hiking clothes that had all the appropriate pockets for my necessary hiking gear.

The ranger began laughing, "That's it! I see you every day in that video!"

We all burst into a moment of contagious laughter about our happenchance meeting that morning. I further explained that our troop did the poses as a service project, and at the time we weren't sure if they would use any of the footage to make the video. It had been well over several years at this point, and I hadn't thought about it since. But there it was in the film, and I reminisced back a few miles while I finished watching the new film thinking, *so time has proven we did make it, and there it is, a living reminder of all our tales and wiles in the park.* What a serendipitous moment, and the perfect start for a 13-mile day hike, with my son's friends, and my new acquaintances.

We had a great day covering the trek in just under nine hours with perfect weather and a leisurely pace. My new hiking partners called my son on our drive back down the mountain, to thank him for the hookup, and tell him about our day. He started out the conversation with, "Max, your mom is my new hero! She got out walking all day and climbing a mountain!" He continued to lament to my son that he couldn't even get his mom to walk to the mailbox.

My son asked his friend to put the phone on speaker, and he replied, "I wanted you to hear this too, Mom; she's my hero too! And thanks, Mom, for taking my friends up the mountain today!"

I choked back the tears of gratitude as I replied, "You are very welcome, and thank you for the opportunity to meet your friends, and to take them on another adventure."

I smiled on the drive home, remembering the real "heroes" in my life, and how they had contributed so much more to my life than I ever gave to them. With all the truest blessings of health, growth, understanding, and awareness. I owe all the profound learning about what is 'truly important in life' to them!

*

One of my all-time favorite quotes is from Sidney Poitier. When he was asked in an interview what his favorite quote was. He replied it was one handed down from his father, who said, "Son, the truest measure of a man is what his children think of him at the end of his life. Not the people who saw him at work, not the people who knew him from a distance, but the people whom he lived with, and was left in the vital care of, and was entrusted with the raising of another human being."

I never forgot that quote, which seemed to imprint my soul when I heard it. Having heard my son's appreciation that day was worth every mountain I'd ever climbed to apprehend this understanding and awareness. Again, I owed this debt of gratitude to the young ladies who challenged me to rise above all my fears and doubts and to see what I was truly capable of by simply going out on a limb where the real fruit truly is!